We Have the Power

A Response to Howard Dean

by

Joan L Green

authorHOUSE™

1663 LIBERTY DRIVE, SUITE 200
BLOOMINGTON, INDIANA 47403
(800) 839-8640
WWW.AUTHORHOUSE.COM

First published by AuthorHouse 03/08/05

ISBN: 1-4208-3329-4 (sc)
ISBN: 1-4208-3328-6 (dj)

Printed in the United States of America
Bloomington, Indiana

This book is printed on acid-free paper.

This book is dedicated to my late husband, who was the best thing to ever happen to my life. Without him, this book would not have become a reality.

I also dedicate this book to my good friends, who understood the pain I was going through while doing my investigation and research and accumulating the material for this book, and stood by me.

Chapter One

In his book, *You Have the Power*, Howard Dean talks about the increasing disparity between the upper and lower economic classes in America and the loss of rights by American citizens. He also points out that we, the American people, have the power to change that disparity and close this gap by using our power at the ballot box. In the last chapter of his book, Howard Dean outlines several reforms that would accomplish this. The reforms he proposes are to restore the balance of power between corporations and American citizens in a democracy, to restore the balance of rights between corporations and citizens, to narrow the wealth gap in capitalism, to create political institutions that people believe in, to create a media that is willing to become a group of watchdogs for Americans and hold politicians accountable, and to stand up against politics of division and fear in America.

I have read Howard Dean's book, and I agree with him on every point, because I have had personal experiences that will substantiate every point he makes. There is just on problem with the solutions he offers. The people do not have the power to close the economic gap that exists between the American public and the corporations by using the ballot box. If it were that simple, it would already have been done. Second, the media cannot and will not be watchdogs for the public. The media, which is supposed to be neutral, runs stories that have shock value because they need ratings. Being watchdogs does not bring ratings; therefore, the media cannot be watchdogs and report for the people. The people have to do this for themselves.

Another problem exists with the two major parties in America. The majority of the officials elected by the people are members of both major political parties. They are elected by and represent the people, yet they take campaign contributions from members of corporate America. One party might get a little more money from an organization than the other party will get, but both parties get contributions from the same groups of people. In addition, top-level executives in corporate America use their lobbyists to assist elected officials in passing laws that are good for corporations and not as good for the general public. Many of these laws actually take rights away from the average American and give financial power to corporations.

Once in office, the elected representatives of the people work closely, probably too closely, with the lobbyists that represent the corporations. These lobbyists work with the people's representatives to rewrite, restructure and add riders to the bills that are introduced into the House. Members of the House and the Senate are supposed to represent the people, but they usually bend to the pressure of corporate lobbyists. We, the people, need to hold our own elected representatives responsible for their actions.

There is a reason the representatives elected by the people are more concerned with the rights of the corporations than the rights of the people. These elected representatives often use their positions of power to boost their careers. An elected official, after serving a term or two in the Congress or Senate, might chose not to run again and opt to become a lobbyist for a DC lobbying firm or get a high-paying job in top-level management in corporate America. This is why the ballot box is not the solution to the problems facing the people of America.

A good solution would be for Howard Dean to leave partisan politics behind and organize and represent the people, who belong to various political parties, to fight for their own rights. The issue of citizens losing their rights to the power of corporate America is not a political one. It is simply an issue of money and power within the Rule of Law.

Laws are supposed to be the result of moral thinking, the edicts of nature and knowledge gained through our life experiences. These laws comprise the Rule of Law, which is a legal principle or fundamental truth that is universally accepted and approved by authorities. This is where we have a problem. If all our laws were truly universally accepted truths, why would America be so disliked around the world?

Laws are supposed to be derived from our experiences in living, but we have very little input into what makes up our laws. Corporate lobbyists can and do have input in DC when our laws are written, voted on and passed. That is, most likely, why laws favor corporate interests and the interests of the wealthy top-level corporate executives. That is also why our laws no longer have to be moral in nature. The content of laws is formed by corporate officers and based on the needs of the corporation for larger profits.

Corporations do not have life experiences to contribute to the law-making process. In addition, corporations are inanimate objects and are not moral in their composition. Corporate executives can use these corporations and their lobbyists for corporate financial gain that deprives American citizens of their rights. It is dangerous for corporations to have more representation in the law-making process than American citizens have. This is where democracy, or government by the people, is lost and fascism begins.

People who vote need to make their elected representatives accountable for their actions. The only way a democracy can be a true democracy is for elected representatives of the people to answer to the people and not the members of corporate management. The officials elected by the people no longer listen to the voice of the people, and they do not truly represent the needs of the people. This has to change to make the democratic process work. There is a way to do this.

When I was young and living in California, many of my representatives in the House and the Senate, on both the state and federal levels, sent out surveys on the issues. These elected officials wanted to know how the public felt about the issues. They asked their constituents to fill out the surveys and return them. The results were compiled, and the elected officials took the results with them when returning to DC or to the state capital. These elected officials listened to the people, and this made the voice of the people part of the democratic process. After these officials voted, they would send out another mailing to their constituents showing the results of the poll. This mailing would contain an explanation of what the majority of the constituents wanted. It would also contain and explanation of the bill that was introduced, how and why the bill was rewritten, how the elected official voted, and why that vote was necessary to carry the voice of the people through the political process. It might be that the constituents wanted a certain bill to pass, but that bill had been rewritten numerous times and contained riders that changed the basis or the bill so much that is was no longer in agreement with what the people wanted. This political process worked once before, and it can work again. We, the people, have to implement it.

We, the people who participated in these surveys, knew we were part of the political process and our voice and our opinion counted. Politicians no longer do this because their loyalty is to the lobbyists from the big corporations. The corporations donated to the candidate's campaigns, and those donations require loyalty. So even though we vote, our voice is seldom, if ever, heard.

Our voice is supposed to be the Rule of Law that governs America. We, the people, are supposed to be the majority that forms the Rule of Law. With our voice being silenced by corporate America, corporations and their need for more profits outweigh our needs, and corporations are making the laws that comprise the Rule of Law and govern America.

Corporations have batteries of lawyers that shield them from consumer complaints, and these lawyers are not kind to people who have legitimate complaints. These lawyers are paid by corporations to not listen to people who have been injured by corporations. These lawyers are hired to get rid of these complaints and push injured people out of the way. This is being done through the Rule of Law in America. If American corporations treat American citizens with such indifference, this is going to become a more serious problem in a global society, with American corporations growing throughout the world and America having so much financial power in the world.

Two major issues being bantered about in the news today, which involve American corporations, are medical malpractice lawsuits asbestosis lawsuits. I find it extremely unusual that President Bush, who claims to be Christian and invokes the name of God in his political dealings, would want to cap lawsuits for people who have been seriously injured by corporations and then injured again by the doctors who do not treat them properly. This is a legal and a moral issue in America, and can easily be compared to fascism, where corporations have complete power over the people, and people are possessions of the state.

The solution to this problem is to give power back to the people. Let the people decide what is right for them. The president, who has not experienced any of the things regarding industrial illness and medical malpractice that I have experienced, should not be allowed to dictate to the people what the laws should be. The laws should reflect the life experiences of the people who live in America.

This book tells my life experiences with industrial illness and medical malpractice. What happened to me will shock those who have not had any experiences in this area. For those who have had similar experiences, I am sure they will be in agreement with me. It was not a pleasant experience for me. I was denied my constitutional rights, just as many other Americans have been denied their rights.

If Americans truly want to regain their rights, there is a legal way to do it. Americans need to have an organization that is truly on their side. Americans need a person to head this organization who will have their best interests at heart. I cannot think of too many high-profile people who would have the ability to do this. After reading his book, I suggest that Howard Dean is this person. He is willing to wage a legal battle for the people against the corporations. He has already expressed his feelings in writing and told Americans that the balance of power between Americans and corporations is now out of balance and needs to be restored. I offer this book to Howard Dean as a challenge to work with and help the people of America.

The type of organization that is needed to help the people has to be determined. I have investigated several types of nonprofit corporations that might be used for this purpose. My idea is to use a 501 (c) 4 corporation for public welfare and model it after the 501 (c) 6 corporation for business leagues. This way people could hire lobbyists that will lobby for their needs and lobby against corporate needs. It will balance the power between American citizens and American corporations. One organization that is a perfect model for the people is Pharmaceutical Research and Manufacturers of America (PhRMA).

PhRMA is a nonprofit corporation and has been used by pharmaceutical companies to get their prescription pills passed by the Food and Drug Administration. PhRMA is a 501 (c) 6, non-profit organization, whose members are officers of publicly traded pharmaceutical manufacturing companies. Each pharmaceutical company that is a member of PhRMA pays thousands of dollars to join and can donate millions to this corporation. None of the donations and memberships are tax deductible, but that does not matter to the pharmaceutical companies that are members. The nonprofit corporation is tax exempt, so all the non-tax deductible dues and contributions of the members can be used by the corporation for lobbying. The object of PhRMA as a business league is to promote the business of the members and get new prescription drugs passed by the Food and Drug Administration (FDA).

A 501 (c) 6 nonprofit organization is an association, such as a business league, chamber of commerce, real estate board, board of trade, or professional football league. A 501 (c) 4 corporation is formed for the public welfare of the people. The dues and the donations would also not be tax deductible, but could be used by the corporation for the purpose of lobbying for the general welfare of the public. This is what the American people need to defend their rights against the attacks of corporate America.

Another issue that would have to be dealt with is the issue of States' Rights and the Uniform Law Commissioners. Each state can make laws independently of other state and the federal government. These laws can vary from state to state, but they must not be in opposition of the U.S. Constitution. This brings into question why we have an organization called The National Conference of Commissioners on Uniform State Laws (NCCUSL).

The NCCUSL was formed in 1892, and funded by the states, based on their population. The members of the NCCUSL are lawyer-legislators, attorneys in private practice, state and federal judges, law professors and legislative staff attorneys. Lawyers, who are members of NCCUSL, have been appointed by state governments and are members of the state bar association. The NCCUSL is self-governed, and the members draft uniform laws that are adopted by the states and support the federal system.

During the last 112 years of the existence of the NCCUSL, the members have drafted more than 250 uniform acts. This makes States' Rights questionable. If the laws of the states are to be uniform, then not many laws can vary. Taking this into consideration, we should ask why doctors are licensed by the states when laws governing doctors must be uniform and support the federal law.

Since the Uniform Law Commissioners accept ideas from private individuals for uniform laws, I will submit my ideas in this book. They will be written in conjunction with my personal experience.

Before I tell my personal experience, I will present two laws written by the NCCUSL and presented to the states to be passed into law. I will show you how these laws affected the hospitalization and death of my husband. In my story, I will show how these laws are being used to violate the federal constitutional rights of Americans. Then I will make recommendations for changes.

The first law drafted by the NCCUSL is the Uniform Determination of Death Act (UDDA), and the second law is the Uniform Anatomical Gift Act (UAGA). There are certain sections of the second law that are very important. In Section 2 (f) (3), the donation can be made through any form of communication, during a terminal illness or injury, addressed to a physician or a surgeon. I'm not a lawyer, but in reading this statement, I interpret that to mean the doctor does not need witnesses. Furthermore, anybody can make this donation. The law is not specific in who has to make the communication. The doctor has the right to take any organs from a person who is terminal, and the doctor does not have to account for who gave him the direction. Furthermore, Section

11 (d) relieves that person of any and all liability for donating another person's organs.

Organ transplant is a moneymaking opportunity in America. It is important for doctors to have our body parts made accessible to them for purposes of research and education as well as transplantation. As you will also see later in my story, the Internal Revenue Service (IRS) governs a hospital's need for organs. In order to qualify as a nonprofit organization, a hospital is divided into three sections. One is patient care, the second is research, and the third is education. The first section of patient care must support both research and education. The IRS code gives the state the right to take our body parts.

The following laws were written to enable doctors and hospitals to follow the IRS code. I am printing these laws, so you can read them and see how they can be used against us. I will also refer to them during my story to show you how they determined what was happening to my husband and how it was being kept from me. These laws show how doctors are shielded from malpractice cases and my story shows how bad doctors are kept in the system.

UNIFORM DETERMINATION OF DEATH ACT

§1. *[Determination of Death.]* An individual 'who has sustained either (1) irreversible cessation of circulatory and respiratory functions, or (2) irreversible cessation of all functions of the entire brain, including the brain stem, is dead. A determination of death must be made in accordance with accepted medical standards.

§2. *[Uniformity of Construction and Application.]* This Act shall be applied and construed to effectuate its general purpose to make uniform the law with respect to the subject of this Act among states enacting it.

§3. *[Short Title.]* This Act may be cited as the Uniform Determination of Death Act.

UNIFORM ANATOMICAL GIFT ACT (1987)

§ 1. Definitions.

As used in this [Act]:

(1) "Anatomical gift" means a donation of all or part of a human body to take effect upon or after death.

(2) "Decedent" means a deceased individual and includes a stillborn infant or fetus.

(3) "Document of gift" means a card, a statement attached to or imprinted on a motor vehicle operator's or chauffeur's license, a will, or other writing used to make an anatomical gift.

(4) "Donor" means an individual who makes an anatomical gift of all or part of the individual's body.

(5) "Enucleator" means an individual who is (Licensed] [certified] by the [State Board of Medical Examiners] to remove or process eyes or parts of eyes.

(6) "Hospital" means a facility licensed, accredited, or approved as a hospital under the law of any state or a facility -operated as a hospital by the United States government, a state, or a subdivision of a state.

(7) "Part" means an organ, tissue, eye, bone, artery, blood, fluid, or other portion of a human body.

(8) "Person" means an individual, corporation, business trust, estate, trust, partner- ship, joint venture, association, government, governmental subdivision or agency, or any other legal or commercial entity.

(9) "Physician" or "surgeon" means an individual licensed or otherwise authorized to practice medicine and surgery or osteopathy and surgery under the laws of any state.

(10) "Procurement organization" means a person licensed, accredited, or approved under the laws of any state for procurement, distribution, or storage of human bodies or parts.

(11) "State" means a state, territory, or possession of the United States, the District of Columbia, or the Commonwealth of Puerto Rico.

(12) "Technician" means an individual who is [licensed] [certified] by the [State Board of Medical Examiners] to remove or process a part.

§ 2. Making, Amending, Revoking, and Refusing to Make Anatomical Gifts by an Individual.

(a) An individual who is at least [18] years of age may (i) make an anatomical gift for any of the purposes stated in Section 6(a), (ii) limit an anatomical gift to one or more of those purposes, or (iii) refuse to make an anatomical gift.

(b) An anatomical gift may be made only by a document of gift signed by the donor. If the donor cannot sign, the document of gift must be signed by another individual and by two witnesses, all of whom have signed at the direction and in the presence of the donor and of each other, and state that it has been so signed.

(c) If a document of gift is attached to or imprinted on a donor's motor vehicle operator's or chauffeur's license, the document of gift must comply with subsection (b). Revocation, suspension, expiration, or cancellation of the license does not invalidate the anatomical gift.

(d) A document of gift may designate a particular physician or surgeon to carry out the appropriate procedures. In the absence of a designation or if the designee is not available, the donee or other person authorized to accept the anatomical gift may employ or authorize any physician, surgeon, technician, or enucleator to carry out the appropriate procedures.

(e) An anatomical gift by will takes effect upon death of the testator, whether or not the will is probated. If, after death, the will is declared invalid for testamentary purposes, the validity of the anatomical gift is unaffected.

(f) A donor may amend or revoke an anatomical gift, not made by will, only by:

(1) a signed statement;

(2) an oral statement made in the presence of two individuals;

(3) any form of communication during a terminal illness or injury addressed to a physician or surgeon; or

(4) the delivery of a signed statement to a specified donee to whom a document of gift had been delivered.

(g) The donor of an anatomical gift made by will may amend or revoke the gift in the manner provided for amendment or revocation of wills, or as provided in subsection (f).

(h) An anatomical gift that is not revoked by the donor before death is irrevocable and does not require the consent or concurrence of any person after the donor's death.

(i) An individual may refuse to make an anatomical gift of the individual's body or part by (i) a writing signed in the same manner as a document of gift, (ii) a statement attached to or imprinted on a donor's motor vehicle operator's or chauffeur's license, or (iii) any other writing used to identify the individual as refusing to make an anatomical gift. During a terminal illness or injury, the refusal may be an oral statement or other form of communication.

(j) In the absence of contrary indications by the donor, an anatomical gift of a part is neither a refusal to give other parts nor a limitation on an anatomical gift under Section 3 or on a removal or release of other parts under Section 4.

(k) In the absence of contrary indications by the donor, a revocation or amendment of an anatomical gift is not a refusal to make another anatomical gift. If the donor intends a revocation to be a refusal to make an anatomical gift, the donor shall make the refusal pursuant to subsection (i).

§ 3. Making, Revoking, and Objecting to Anatomical Gifts, by Others.

(a) Any member of the following classes of persons, in the order of priority listed, may make an anatomical gift of all or a part of the decedent's body for an authorized purpose, unless the decedent, at the time of death, has made an unrevoked refusal to make that anatomical gift:

(1) the spouse of the decedent;

(2) an adult son or daughter of the decedent,

(3) either parent of the decedent;

(4) an adult brother or sister of the decedent;

(5) a grandparent of the decedent; and

(6) a guardian of the person of the decedent at the time of death.

(b) An anatomical gift may not be made by a person listed in subsection (a) if:

(1) a person in a prior class is available at the time of death to make an anatomical gift;

(2) the person proposing to make an anatomical gift knows of a refusal or contrary indications by the decedent; or

(3) the person proposing to make an anatomical gift knows of an objection to making an anatomical gift by a member of the person's class or a prior class.

(c) An anatomical gift by a person authorized under subsection (a) must be made by (i) a document of gift signed by the person or (ii) the person's telegraphic, recorded telephonic, or other recorded message, or other form of communication from the person that is contemporaneously reduced to writing and signed by the recipient.

(d) An anatomical gift by a person authorized under subsection (a) may be revoked by any member of the same or a prior class if, before procedures have begun for the removal of a part from the body of the decedent, the physician, surgeon, technician, or enucleator removing the part knows of the revocation.

(e) A failure to make an anatomical gift under subsection (a) is not an objection to the making of an anatomical gift.

§ 4. Authorization by [Coroner] [Medical Examiner] or [Local Public Health Official].

(a) The [coroner] [medical examiner] may release and permit the removal of a part from a body within that official's custody, for transplantation or therapy, if:

(1) the official has received a request for the part from a hospital, physician, surgeon, or procurement organization;

(2) the official has made a reasonable effort, taking into account the useful life of the part, to locate and examine the decedent's medical records and inform persons listed in Section 3(a) of their option to make, or object to making, an anatomical gift;

(3) the official does not know of a refusal or contrary indication by the decedent or objection by a person having priority to act as listed in Section 3(a);

(4) the removal will be by a physician, surgeon, or technician; but in the case of eyes, by one of them or by an enucleator;

(5) the removal will not interfere with any autopsy or investigation;

(6) the removal will be in accordance with accepted medical standards; and

(7) cosmetic restoration will be done, if appropriate.

(b) If the body is not within the custody of the [coroner] [medical examiner], the [local public health officer] may release and permit the removal of any part from a body in the [local public health officer's] custody for transplantation or therapy if the requirements of subsection (a) are met.

(c) An official releasing and permitting the removal of a part shall maintain a permanent record of the name of the decedent, the person making the request, the date and purpose of the request, the part requested, and the person to whom it was released.

§ 5. Routine Inquiry and Required Request; Search and Notification.

(a) On or before admission to a hospital, or as soon as possible thereafter, a person designated by the hospital shall ask each patient who is at least [18] years of age: "Are you an organ or tissue donor?" If the answer is affirmative the person shall request a copy of the document of gift. If the answer is negative or there, is no answer and the attending physician consents, the person designated shall discuss with the patient the option to make or refuse to make an anatomical gift. The answer to the question, an available copy of any document of gift or refusal to make an anatomical gift, and any other relevant information, must be placed in the patient's medical record.

(b) If, at or near the time of death of a patient, there is no medical record that the patient has made or refused to make an anatomical gift, the hospital [administrator] or a representative designated by the (administrator] shall discuss the option to make or refuse to make an anatomical gift and request the making of an anatomical gift pursuant to Section 3(a). The request must be made with reasonable discretion and sensitivity to the circumstances of the family. A request is not required if the gift is not suitable, based upon accepted medical standards, for a purpose specified in Section 6. An entry must be made in the medical record of the patient, stating the name and affiliation of the individual making the request, and of the name, response, and relationship to the patient of the person to whom the request was made. The [Commissioner of Health] shall [establish guidelines] [adopt regulations] to implement this subsection.

(c) The following persons shall make a reasonable search for a document of gift or other information identifying the bearer as a donor or as an individual who has refused to make an anatomical gift:

(1) a law enforcement officer, fireman, paramedic, or other emergency rescuer finding an individual who the searcher believes is dead or near death; and

(2) a hospital, upon the admission of an individual at or near the time of death, if there is not immediately available any other source of that information.

(d) If a document of gift or evidence of refusal to make an anatomical gift is located by the search required by subsection (c)(1), and the individual or body to whom it relates is taken to a hospital, the hospital must be notified of the contents and the document or other evidence must be sent to the hospital.

(e) If, at or near the time of death of a patient, a hospital knows that an anatomical gift has been made pursuant to Section 3(a) or a release and removal of a part has been permitted pursuant to Section 4, or that a patient or an individual identified as in transit to the hospital is a donor, the hospital shall notify the donee if one is named and known to the hospital; if not, it shall notify an appropriate procurement organization. The hospital shall cooperate in the implementation of the anatomical gift or release and removal of a part.

(f) A person who fails to discharge the duties imposed by this section is not subject to criminal or civil liability but is subject to appropriate administrative sanctions.

§ 6. Persons Who May Become Donees; Purposes for Which Anatomical Gifts may be Made.

(a) The following persons may become donees of anatomical gifts for the purposes stated:

(1) a hospital, physician, surgeon, or procurement organization, for transplantation, therapy, medical or dental education, research, or advancement of medical or dental science;

(2) an accredited medical or dental school, college, or university for education, research, advancement of medical or dental science; or

(3) a designated individual for transplantation or therapy needed by that individual.

(b) An anatomical gift may be made to a designated donee or without designating a donee. If a donee is not designated or if the donee is not available or rejects the anatomical gift, the anatomical gift may be accepted by any hospital.

(c) If the donee knows of the decedent's refusal or contrary indications to make an anatomical gift or that an anatomical gift by a member of a class having priority to act is opposed by a member of the same class or a prior class under Section 3(a), the donee may not accept the anatomical gift.

Subsection (e) incorporates a recommendation of The Task Force Report pursuant to the National Organ Transplant Act of 1984 that "The Commission for Uniform State Laws develop model legislation that requires acute care hospitals to develop an affiliation with an organ procurement agency and to adopt routine inquiry policies and procedures." The present draft incorporates this recommendation in Sections 5 and 9.

Subsection (f) encourages hospital accrediting agencies, law enforcement, and other state agencies that have existing disciplinary procedures to impose sanctions for failure to discharge the duties imposed by Section 5.

§ 7. Delivery of Document of Gift.

(a) Delivery of a document of gift during the donor's lifetime is not required for the validity of an anatomical gift.

(b) If an anatomical gift is made to a designated donee, the document of gift, or a copy, may be delivered to the donee to expedite the appropriate procedures after death. The document of gift, or a copy, may be deposited in any hospital, procurement organization, or registry office that accepts it for safekeeping or for facilitation of procedures after death. On request of an interested person, upon or after the donor's death, the person in possession shall allow the interested person to examine or copy the document of gift.

§ 8. Rights and Duties at Death.

(a) Rights of a donee created by an anatomical gift are superior to rights of others except with respect to autopsies under Section 11(b). A donee may accept or reject an anatomical gift. If a donee accepts an anatomical gift of an entire body, the donee, subject to the terms of the gift, may allow embalming and use of the body in funeral services. If the gift is of a part of a body, the donee, upon the death of the donor and before embalming, shall cause the part to be removed without unnecessary mutilation. After removal of the part, custody of the remainder of the body vests in the person under obligation to dispose of the body.

(b) The time of death must be determined by a physician or surgeon who attends the donor at death or, if none, the physician or surgeon who certifies the death. Neither the physician or surgeon who attends the donor at death nor the physician or surgeon who determines the time of death may participate in the procedures for removing or trans- planting a part unless the document of gift designates a particular physician or surgeon pursuant to Section 2(d).

(e) If there has been an anatomical gift, a technician may remove any donated parts and an enucleator may remove any donated eyes or parts of eyes, after determination of death by a physician or surgeon.

§ 9. Coordination of Procurement and Use.

Each hospital in this State, after consultation with other hospitals and procurement organizations, shall establish agreements or affiliations for coordination of procurement and use of human bodies and parts.

§ 10. Sale or Purchase of Parts Prohibited.

(a) A person may not knowingly, for valuable consideration, purchase or sell a part for transplantation or therapy, if removal of the part is intended to occur after the death of the decedent.

(b) Valuable consideration does not include reasonable payment for the removal, processing, disposal, preservation, quality control, storage, transportation, or implantation of a part.

(c) A person who violates this section is guilty of a [felony] and upon conviction is subject to a fine not exceeding [$50,000] or imprisonment not exceeding [five] years, or both.

§ 11. Examination, Autopsy, Liability.

(a) An anatomical gift authorizes any reasonable examination necessary to assure medical acceptability of the gift for the purposes intended.

(b) The provisions of this [Act] are subject to the laws of this State governing autopsies.

(c) A hospital, physician, surgeon, [coroner], [medical examiner), [local public health officer], enucleator, technician, or other person, who acts in accordance with this [Act] or with the applicable anatomical gift law of another state [or a foreign country] or attempts in good faith to do so is not liable for that act in a civil action or criminal proceeding.

(d) An individual who makes an anatomical gift pursuant to Section 2 or 3 and the individual's estate are not liable for any injury or damage that may result from the making or the use of the anatomical gift.

§ 12. Transitional Provisions.

This [Act] applies to a document of gift, revocation, or refusal to make an anatomical gift signed by the donor or a person authorized to make or object to making an anatomical gift before, on, or after the effective date of this [Act].

§ 13. Uniformity of Application and Construction.

This [Act] shall be applied and construed to effectuate its general purpose to make uniform the law with respect to the subject of this [Act] among states enacting it.

§ 14. Severability.

If any provision of this [Act] or its application thereof to any person or circumstance is held invalid, the invalidity does not affect other provisions or applications of this [Act] which can be given effect without the invalid provision or application, and to this end the provisions of this [Act] are severable.

§ 15. Short Title.

This [Act] may be cited as the "Uniform Anatomical Gift Act (1987)."

Chapter Two

In recent years, many lawsuits have been filed against corporate America due to the physical injury and death caused by industrial illnesses. The main focus is on illness and death caused by asbestosis, but there are many other products used in industry that cause disease and industrial illness. Now, President Bush wants to eliminate these lawsuits, because they are affecting the profits of corporations. He also wants to eliminate medical malpractice complaints and lawsuits. The real solution to medical malpractice cases is to get bad doctors out of the system. The solution to industrial illness would be to make corporations stop using products that cause these illnesses or make corporations maintain safety standards when employees perform work around these products.

It also might be better for the country if President Bush were to act like the true Christian he claims to be and propose laws that would make corporations pay for the care of the people who were injured, rather than stop the lawsuits or have cover ups. Christianity is more than just keeping the words "Under God" in the pledge of Allegiance or saying "God Bless You" a the end of a speech. A true Christian also does not make determinations about people based on money and power. George Bush might do well to keep in mind this message from the bible, in Matthew 25:35-40,

"The King will reply, 'I tell you the truth, whatever you did for one of the least of these brothers of mine, you did for me.'" My husband did not deserve to die the way he did, and I hope and pray George Bush will stop others from dying in the same way in American hospitals.

In America, profits and high salaries for corporate executives take precedence over caring for injured workers. My story is so important because it proves that doctors' careers and corporate dollars are more valuable in America that the life of American citizens. I'm telling this story so people will become aware of this critical situation. We need to have someone in this country who will look out for the rights of the people. We need an organization that is powerful and will help us. One person, by his or herself, cannot possibly fight corporate America. The laws are written so that it is very difficult, and often impossible, to even get cases in court. This is why I'm challenging Howard Dean to unite with the average people and help us regain our rights and make a difference in America.

* * *

My husband became ill in the fall of 1998, but my story actually began years before that time. We had been married for 16 years, and not too long after we were married, my husband revealed his prior work background and his exposure to asbestos, silica and many chemical agents and solvents. Prior to our being married, he had worked for the Sheetmetal Workers Local. At the time we were married, he worked for the US Department of Defense (DoD), and he was still working around chemicals and solvents involved in the repair of aircraft, including silica, which is contained in welding rods. I also found out later that the water used when working with sheetmetal can be contaminated and can cause industrial illness, such as strange bacterial infections. My husband had also been in Desert Shield and Desert Storm and was awarded a civilian meritorious unit commendation for his work on military aircraft.

My husband already knew he had done a lot of damage to his body, but he still felt he was alive and well, except for some severe pains, so he figured everything was going to be all right for him. For many years he complained of joint pain, but it could not be attributed to any particular ailment. Later, after he retired from DoD, he did have a bout with bronchitis. After reading about industrial illness, I found out that many symptoms can appear over a period of time that could be as long as 30 years or more. The destruction done to the body and the pulmonary system takes years before it is recognized. Whether it is discovered early or late in life makes no difference. Industrial illness is most always terminal.

After reading about Silica, I found out that when it comes into contact with the lung tissue for a long period of time, it leaves the lung tissue irreversibly thickened and scarred, which is a condition known as fibrosis. It takes years of exposure before this disease and the damage it causes becomes noticeable to the person who has it. The result is that the lungs cannot supply oxygen to the blood as well as they should be able to. A cough and a shortness of breath are also associated with this disease. My husband did not develop the cough until the summer of 1998. At that time, the doctor discovered there was a lack of oxygen in his blood. For many years he had sleep problems as well as pain in his joints. In later years he had noticed the shortness of breath, and that is why we walked more than a mile every morning for about five years before he became seriously ill. He felt the walking helped him. Toward the end, he did have all the symptoms: chest pain, fatigue, malaise, and loss of appetite. He was diagnosed by the doctor with lung fibrosis and with having a loss of oxygen in his blood.

There is no cure for Silicosis. Smoking cigarettes can aggravate the disease, but smoking does not cause the disease. Having the disease increases the risk of pneumoccoccal infection, a common cause of pneumonia. The damage caused by silicosis can lead to lung infections, such as bacterial infections and TB.

My husband had retired from the Department of Defense (DoD), and we moved to Las Vegas, Nevada. He took a job in a hotel and casino in the Las Vegas area and worked there until he became ill. At first he thought it was only a bout with pneumonia, since many other hotel employees has recently been diagnosed with having pneumonia.

The doctor took X-rays and found scarring plus black spots covering of his entire left lung and half of the right lung. The diagnosis at this point was black lung disease, which is industrial illness. My husband and the doctor discussed my husband's work history and decided it had to have a connection with the welding he had done over the years, because welding rods have silica in them, or with the asbestos he had worked with. The doctor also thought the chemicals could have exacerbated the illness.

Silica seemed to be a more obvious conclusion than asbestos. Silica consists of transparent, tasteless crystals found in certain rocks; among them are agate, amethyst, sand and quartz. These compounds are ground up for industrial uses and are insoluble in water or acids. The amount of dust or crystals inhaled influences the seriousness of the injury to the lung. Macrophages, or white blood vessels, in the lungs ingest small, dust particles as they are inhaled. The macrophages die after they swallow the dust particles, and they give off toxic substances that cause the scar tissue to form. An excess amount of dust in the lungs can cause too many macrophages to die off and result in bacterial disease forming in the lungs.

The cause of silicosis my husband and I could identify and associate with his condition was the silica that is used in welding rods. Most of his career, he worked with sheetmetal and did welding and repairs on aircraft. He had worked for the Sheetmetal Workers Union and the U.S. Department of Defense. My husband had also done a lot of welding on various occasions when he worked for a chemical company. This combination of chemicals and welding can also do severe damage to the lung tissue. In addition, he did have contact with asbestos when he worked on cars. Even with all the industrial contact he had, the one that seemed to fit his condition was Silicosis.

This doctor told my husband he could not care for him and he had to find a pulmonary physician. We went in search of one, which was not easy. They all seem so opposed to even thinking a person would have an industrial illness. We did locate an office where all the doctors specialized in pulmonary diseases and illness, and the doctor there seemed certain my husband's condition was work-related.

After administering many tests, the pulmonary specialist decided my husband needed a bronchoscopy. He said that was the only way we would find out exactly what was wrong. The decision to have the bronchoscopy was the biggest mistake we ever made. My husband walked into the hospital as an outpatient that day, but did not walk out.

A week later, he was sent home and told he had to stay in bed and have home healthcare. Later, when I looked at the medical records, I discovered he had contracted VRE when he was in the hospital. That meant he was terminal. VRE is a highly contagious bacterial infection that is resistant to antibiotics. The doctors and the hospital never told me about the VRE. If I had not purchased my husband's medical records, I would never have found out about it. I found it hard to believe that the doctor risked my life and the lives of the home healthcare personnel by sending him home. It appeared to me that the doctors did not know what to do and did not want to be bothered with industrial disease, so they sent him home not caring who he infected with the VRE he had contracted while in the hospital. It was shocking for me to discover how irresponsible and uncaring healthcare workers can be in this country.

There are some very important pages in the medical records that I have to share with the readers. The first one is a pathology report that shows two kinds of RARE findings and Vancomyecin Resistant Enterococci. These three items are important. The first two show that what my husband had was identified as RARE by the pathologists. The third item shows that my husband had contracted a deadly bacterial infection while in the hospital. The first two items on the pathology report show that my husband's illness was rare and not a normal or average illness. The third item shows that my husband was already marked as a dead man.

```
                    *** DAILY LAB SUMMARY REPORT ***
                            05/17/99   0100


Pt Name:  GREEN,WILLIAM P                                   D.E447-0

                               NONE

  Col Date Time Specimen #       Source      Sp Desc   P/F Organisms ...
> 05/13/99 1935 99:SZ:B0016228R  URINE       RANDOM     P  VREFM
```

*** BACTERIOLOGY ***

```
SPEC #: 99:SZ:B0016061R    COLL: 05/12/99-0900    STATUS: COMP        REQ #: 02116029
                           RECD: 05/12/99-1058    SUBM DR: ████████
SOURCE: BRON WASH
SPDESC: LT UP LOBE

ORDERED:  GRAM STAIN, BRONCH CULT

  GRAM STAIN   Final 05/12/99
       GRAM STAIN                 MODERATE WHITE BLOOD CELLS
                               / FEW GRAM POSITIVE COCCI
                               / RARE EPITHELIAL CELLS


SPEC #: 99:SZ:B0016063R    COLL: 05/12/99-0900    STATUS: COMP        REQ #: 02116033
                           RECD: 05/12/99-1102    SUBM DR: ████████
SOURCE: BRONCH LAV
SPDESC: LT UP LOBE

ORDERED:  GRAM STAIN, BRONCH CULT

  GRAM STAIN   Final 05/12/99
       GRAM STAIN                 MODERATE WHITE BLOOD CELLS
                               / RARE GRAM POSITIVE COCCI
```

*** URINE CULTURE ***

```
SPEC #: 99:SZ:B0016228R    COLL: 05/13/99-1935    STATUS: RES         REQ #: 02119495
                           RECD: 05/13/99-2115    SUBM DR: ████████
SOURCE: URINE
SPDESC: RANDOM

ORDERED:  URINE CULT

  CULTURE URINE W/COLONY COUNT  Preliminary
       COLONY COUNT ORGANISM #1    >100,000 CFU/ML

    Organism 1                 ENTERO FAECIUM, VANCO RESIS
```

```
 Pt Name:   GREEN,WILLIAM P
 Attend Dr: ████████
 Acct#:     D00080584956   Age/Sex:  61/M
 Unit#:     D001153751     Status:   ADM IN
 Adm Date:  05/12/99       Dis Date:              LABORATORY DAILY SUMMARY
```

After approximately a week of being home, my husband could not catch his breath. I called the home healthcare specialists, and the nurse told me to call 911 immediately. I did so, and my husband was taken by ambulance and readmitted to the hospital. I kept trying to talk to the doctor about my husband's illness, but he avoided me by saying he was not supposed to talk to me, which I thought was strange because my husband told me the doctor's would not talk to him about his illness either. My husband also begged me to find out what had happened to him.

I finally did get to talk to the doctor, and I asked him if there was anything that could be done. I asked him if surgery was an option. The doctor told me that because there was so much damage to the lungs, my husband was not able to have surgery. He also said that my husband would surely die during surgery. I then asked him if my husband would get well. I did not know about the VRE at that time, and the doctor did not tell me. He just said that my husband's illness could go either way. He could die or he could get well at any time. That was a lie, and now I know it. How cruel it was for a doctor to tell me something like that, giving me hope that my husband might recover. He was never going to recover from VRE, and his pulmonary illness only added to the odds that he would not recover. The only truth the doctor did tell me was that surgery would kill him.

I then asked if there was another hospital that might offer better and more advanced antibiotics that would help him. I figured that since the doctor had said my husband could recover maybe stronger antibiotics would be the answer. The doctor then made arrangements for another hospital to review his records. The staff at that hospital had access to everything that I did not know at that time. They knew about the VRE and the pulmonary problems. In fact, they knew that my husband's doctor had his condition listed as respiratory failure. That, according to the law, meant my husband was terminal. It would have taken a lung transplant to save him, but my husband was 61, and that is considered to be too old to try and save a life. A child would have better options than a man of 61.

If you go back and look at the Uniform Determination of Death Act (UDDA), you will that doctors consider a person dead when he or she has irreversible cessation of circulatory and respiratory functions. I believe that is the same as respiratory failure. I had no idea at that time exactly how close to death my husband was, and the doctors would not tell me the truth.

There is another pathology report that is important. It is a consultation done by a doctor at the hospital my husband was transferred to. I found this to be highly unusual, because my husband was transferred to the very hospital this doctor works for, and this doctor never mentioned that fact in the medical records. Furthermore, this doctor worked on my husband's case by assisting another pathologist. Failing to mention in the hospital records that he had previously consulted on my husband's case is highly irregular. A doctor should always disclose any prior dealings he or she has had with a patient.

Joan L Green

ANATOMIC PATHOLOGY REPORT

PATIENT: GREEN, WILLIAM P
SPECIMEN #: SZ:S99-6876
Physician:

Collected: 05/12/99
Received: 05/12/99
Accessioned: 05/12/99

ADDENDUM FINDINGS

Addendum #2   **Entered: 05/20/99-1234**

Outside consultation was received from Dr. [redacted] at the [redacted] Dr. [redacted] diagnosis was biopsy of left upper lobe showing chronic inflammation and non-necrotizing granulomas, mycobacterial infection is favored. He indicated that although there is some background birefringent material he did not think it was present in sufficient amounts to allow any more specific comments and that it could be the residual residue of cigarette smoking or occupational exposure. He did not think this is a sort of biopsy that would be useful in pursuing further to address a question of pneumoconiosis in this patient.   (DPK/tcg)

*/A

Dictated by:

Addendum Prelim: *05/20/99

32

The new hospital reviewed his case and gave me more hope. My husband was accepted as a patient. He was scheduled to be flown in an ambulance plane to the new hospital on a Friday afternoon. I went home and packed a bag for him. Besides putting in pajamas and underwear, I put all the paperwork the lawyers had drawn up in the bag. There was a copy of his will, his healthcare directives and his power of attorney for health care decisions that named me as attorney in fact. At that time I did not know that anyone in respiratory failure should not be transported by air, and I do not know why the doctors allowed this to happen. The following image shows what the doctors knew what I did not know.

Joan L Green

PHYSICIAN CERTIFICATE FOR TRANSFER

PATIENT NAME: *William Green* (the "Patient") MEDICAL RECORD # : D0011537

As the Patient's attending physician and the transferring physician, I hereby certify that I have examined the Patient an based on the information available at this time, the medical benefits reasonably expected from the provision of appropria medical treatment at ███████████ (the "Receiving Facility") outweigh the increased risks to the Patient by not being transferred and, in the case of labor, the unborn child.

The following is a summary of the risks upon which this certificate is based: _____

1. Possible intractable respiratory failure

2. Severe Cardiac problem

The following is a summary of the benefits upon which this certificate is based: _____

1. Patient failing despite all treatment & diagnostic efforts. Without pursuit without prolonged Care by national experts.

This certificate for transfer was not necessitated as a result of an on-call physician having refused or failed to appe within a reasonable time to provide necessary stabilizing treatment.

DATE: 6/4/99 TIME: _____

████████████
TRANSFERRING PHYSICIAN   CONSULTING PHYSICIAN (if any)

PATIENT IDENTIFICATION   ROOM #

GREEN, WILLIAM P
DOB 09171937   M/61   CAT   LRM

34

I came back to the hospital with my husband's duffle bag, and he asked me to ride with him on the flight to the new hospital. The doctor informed us that my husband would have to be sedated put on a respirator for the flight out of state. I asked if he would remain on the respirator after arriving at the new hospital. The doctor assured me it was only for the flight. He said my husband would be taken off the respirator and allowed to wake up from the sedatives. While they were getting my husband ready for the flight, I was told I could not ride on the flight with him because there was not enough room for me. I was standing outside the door to my husband's room and the door was slightly ajar. The nurses were working to insert the tube for the respirator. My husband had been sedated, but evidently something was not agreeing with him, because he was moving around a lot. I then saw a hand go up and slap him on the face. I was already upset, and I did not know what to do. I started toward the open door, when it was pushed closed from the inside. I thought it would be best not to say anything since my husband was on his way out of that hospital.

Since I was not allowed on the ambulance plane, I called my sister and asked if she and her husband would come and get me and take me to the new hospital. They said they would come to Las Vegas and get me just as soon as they could. My husband was already sedated and on the respirator, so I left my husband's duffle bag with him for the flight, and I returned home to pack a bag for myself.

Chapter Three

I found out that my sister and her husband were not going to be able to come for me until late in the weekend or the beginning of the following week. I started placing calls to the new hospital, hoping to talk to my husband. It was late Friday before he arrived at the hospital, and this is also when I discovered he was being kept sedated and on the respirator. I was upset because it was my understanding that he would be taken off the respirator and would not be kept sedated. I asked to talk to the doctor in charge, but nobody seemed to want to speak with me. I then asked the nurse about my husband's duffle bag, and they said there was no bag with him. I left my home and cell numbers, hoping the doctor would call me. The next morning, I went back to the hospital in Las Vegas and found the duffle bag still sitting in his room. They never bothered to take his duffle bag, which contained all his legal paperwork.

Chapter Four

The hospital records state that a doctor, whom I will call Dr. # 1, was the attending physician when my husband arrived by ambulance plane. He did two things that surprised me. First he wrote in the medical records that no family history could be obtained. I don't know why. I called the hospital several times, but no doctor would speak to me. I could have supplied the family history. Furthermore, the doctor could not get a systems review because my husband had been left sedated on the respirator, even though I had been told he would be taken off the respirator and not kept sedated. I was concerned about this because my husband had been awake and talking to me before he was put in the respirator for the flight. The following report indicates that Dr. # 1 did not bother with attempting to get the family history.

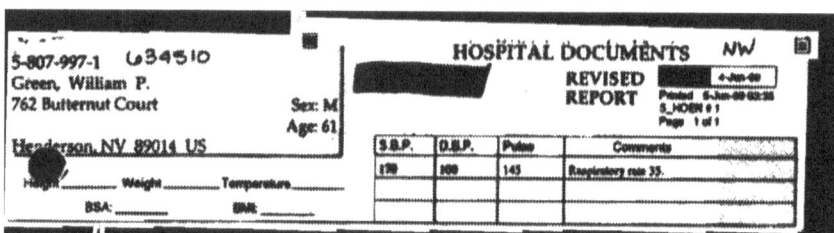

5-807-997-1   634510
Green, William P.
762 Butternut Court   Sex: M
                                             Age: 61
Henderson, NV 89014 US

Height _____ Weight _____ Temperature _____
BSA: _____   BMI: _____

HOSPITAL DOCUMENTS   NW
REVISED   4-Jun-99
REPORT   Printed 6-Jun-99 03:35
                         S_HOEN # 1
                         Page 1 of 1

S.B.P.	D.B.P.	Pulse	Comments
170	100	145	Respiratory rate 35.

4-Jun-99

M.D.
2-5643
CC-H
HHP
9A2

CHIEF COMPLAINT/PURPOSE OF VISIT:
HOSPITAL HISTORY AND PHYSICAL.

CHIEF COMPLAINT: Transfer for tertiary care.

HISTORY OF PRESENT ILLNESS:
This 61-year-old male has a history of progressive dyspnea over the past one year. This has been progressive in nature and has reached the point where he is no longer able to work. He has been followed in Las Vegas, Nevada, by a pulmonologist who performed a CT scan of the chest on March 22, 1999. This revealed severe emphysema with extensive left upper lobe consolidation and mild bilateral interstitial infiltrates. There are also some lymph nodes in the chest. His condition progressed to the point where he underwent a bronchoscopy on 05/12/99 and required hospital admission following this. The bronchoscopy revealed negative cultures except there was a positive AFB. This apparently was not a mycobacterium tuberculosis by RNA study. Apparently, cultures are still pending. Bacterial and fungal cultures were negative and the cytology was apparently unremarkable at that time. The patient was discharged on home O2 and apparently returned with progressive respiratory problems on 05/29/99. He was readmitted to the hospital and his chest x-ray showed worsening of his pulmonary infiltrates. The patient has been treated with antituberculin drugs including ethambutol, rifabutin, INH, and PZA. He was started on steroids 06/03/99, one day prior to his transfer to this facility. The patient was transferred to the Mayo Clinic Hospital at family request, for tertiary care. He was intubated at the other hospital prior to his transfer and was brought by air ambulance to Scottsdale Airport. He was apparently given intravenous sedation prior to his transfer and was given intravenous muscle relaxants in the aircraft to keep him from moving about.

PAST MEDICAL/SURGICAL HISTORY
His past medical history is apparently positive for hypertension, although he apparently is not taking any medications for this at the present time.

ALLERGIES:
No known drug allergies.

SOCIAL HISTORY:
Apparently, this patient has a 45-pack-year history and apparently he stopped smoking two weeks ago. He has a history of exposure to asbestos and sandblasting dust. The patient also has some remote history of radiation exposure.

FAMILY HISTORY:
Could not be obtained.

CURRENT MEDICATIONS:
His medications at the time of transfer were amikacin, clindamycin, Biaxin, Cipro, ethambutol, rifabutin, Theo-dur, and Solu-Medrol. He was also taking albuterol by nebulized inhalers.

SYSTEMS REVIEW:
Review of systems could not be obtained because the patient was intubated.

PHYSICAL EXAMINATION:
Physical examination at the time of his arrival in the Intensive Care Unit: The patient was afebrile.
GENERALLY: The patient appeared to be in moderate distress and was intubated.
HEENT: Exam revealed the pupils to be quite small and constricted and nonreactive. An oral tracheal tube was in place and a nasogastric tube was in place. There was no mass in the neck and no cervical adenopathy noted. There was no thyromegaly and the trachea was midline.
CHEST: The patient had very distant breath sounds but they appeared to be equal with bagging.
CARDIOVASCULAR EXAM: The heart rate was irregular and quite fast. There was an S3 gallop. There was no murmur heard.
ABDOMEN: The abdomen was soft and not tender and a few bowel sounds were heard. There were no masses palpated and the liver could not be palpated.
EXTREMITIES: There was no peripheral edema and the patient had 3+ pulses in all extremities.
NEUROLOGIC EXAM: The patient did not respond to verbal stimuli. The patient became somewhat agitated with painful stimuli. There were no obvious focal neurologic deficits noted.

IMPRESSION/REPORT/PLAN:
LABORATORY: The white blood count was 14,000, and the hemoglobin was 11. The platelet count was 300,000. The sodium was 143 and the potassium was 4.5. The BUN was 20 and the creatinine was 0.7. Albumin was 2.5. Arterial blood

The next surprise was that Dr. # 1 recommended surgery. He stated he would consult with the thoracic department, but there were no notes of a consultation in the medical records. Furthermore, there were not notes by anyone else recommending the surgery. It was just the word of Dr. # 1. My home and cellular numbers were written on this form and were part of the medical records, yet no doctor ever attempted to call me. Then Dr. # 1 ordered the surgery. My husband's doctor in Las Vegas had told me that my husband would die if he had surgery. That is why my husband was transferred for managed treatment with antibiotics. Now, Dr. # 1 orders surgery. I did not know at that time that anybody was even thinking about surgery or recommending it for my husband. I still could not get any doctor to talk to me.

This is taken from the medical records and shows that Dr. # 1 was going to talk to the thoracic department and request surgery. I think it is very peculiar that the head of the thoracic department never wrote anything regarding this issue. The head of the thoracic department had to be notified, or the surgery could not have been done. I just do not understand why he did not bother to write anything in the medical records.

I do not know anything for sure, but I did wonder if maybe the head of the thoracic department knew this was not a good surgery and did not want to be involved, but still allowed it to go forth. The head of the thoracic department had to know that my husband would die in surgery. He also had to know that my husband should never have been moved to that hospital because he was in respiratory failure. He had to know that my husband would not withstand the anesthesia. The head of the thoracic department was a doctor who earned close to $500,000 a year. To earn that salary, I assumed he had to be a fairly intelligent person who knew the facts. So, the question remains, why would he allow the surgery to ahead. Was it out of his hands? Did the order come from someone higher? Was there a need for the lung tissue? I'll never know the answer to any of these questions.

Following is the hospital report that shows how Dr. # 1 requested the surgery, but there were no other notes from any other doctor making any comments about whether or not the surgery should be performed.

Progress Notes Require Date, Signature, & Pager No. Residents *must* also print their name.

Date, Time, Sign, & Include Pager # on all Notes	
6/5/99	Full Note to be Dictated.
	Asked by Dr. ▓▓▓▓▓ for Pulm consult.
Pulm	61 y/o man with hx of asbestos, probably silica exposure.
HC-3	Long hx smoking, hx of pet birds at home.
2-7830	One year of progressive DOE; months of night sweats, wt loss
	Found locally to have bil. int. lung disease, focal LUL
	consolidation. Bronch 5/12 – AFB ⊕ M+bg genprobe ⊖
	No real improvement. Transferred to MCO on ventilator
	Diff Dx includes:
	IRF, Mycobacterium avium complex (MAC) infection,
	Asbestosis, Silicosis, Alveolar proteinosis, Nonrsha
	Hypersensitivity Pneumonitis, etc.
	Suggest: PThienbutol, Rifabin, Levaquin should be
	appropriate antibiotic Rx empirically at this time.
	I think he needs a diagnostic open lung bx send
	for full cultures and path because of the diff dx
	listed above.
	Doubt mycobacterium tuberculosum.
	I have contacted Thoracic Surgery to request
	consultation for ⓁL-sided diagnostic OLBx.
	Would D/C Theophylline
	add 0.5mg Atrovent to
	albuterol treatments. 2-7830
6/5/99	CCS
	will ask Infectious Disease
	to eval as well.
	wife tele #
	H 702-450-0392
	cellular 702-521-1281
	Joan Green

Chapter Five

The next doctor to enter this confusing picture is Dr. # 2. He arranged a telephone consent for an inpatient surgery, that was not an emergency, but he still did not call me, the patient's wife. I am still very suspicious about this. The law in every state lists the order of priorities, and the wife is always the person to give consent. Now, why would this doctor make a telephone call to someone else, and not even list that person's phone number in the medical records. That appears very suspicious to me.

This Informed Patient Consent shows the consent form signed by Dr. # 2 and witnessed by a nurse, using a printed name for a telephone consent, from someone other than the patient's wife.

Joan L Green

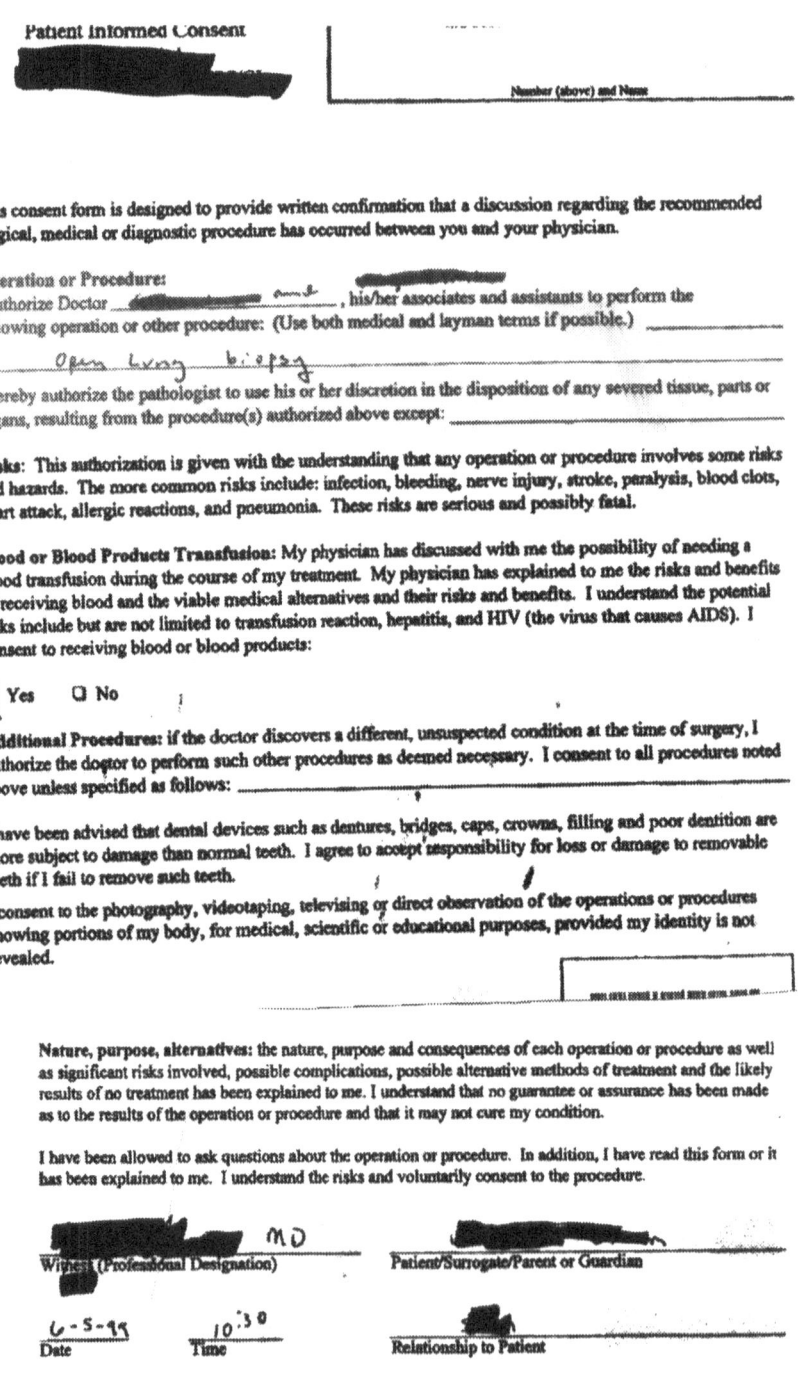

Patient Informed Consent

Number (above) and Name

This consent form is designed to provide written confirmation that a discussion regarding the recommended surgical, medical or diagnostic procedure has occurred between you and your physician.

Operation or Procedure:
I authorize Doctor _____ and _____, his/her associates and assistants to perform the following operation or other procedure: (Use both medical and layman terms if possible.) _____

_____ Open Lung biopsy

I hereby authorize the pathologist to use his or her discretion in the disposition of any severed tissue, parts or organs, resulting from the procedure(s) authorized above except: _____

Risks: This authorization is given with the understanding that any operation or procedure involves some risks and hazards. The more common risks include: infection, bleeding, nerve injury, stroke, paralysis, blood clots, heart attack, allergic reactions, and pneumonia. These risks are serious and possibly fatal.

Blood or Blood Products Transfusion: My physician has discussed with me the possibility of needing a blood transfusion during the course of my treatment. My physician has explained to me the risks and benefits of receiving blood and the viable medical alternatives and their risks and benefits. I understand the potential risks include but are not limited to transfusion reaction, hepatitis, and HIV (the virus that causes AIDS). I consent to receiving blood or blood products:

☒ Yes   ☐ No

Additional Procedures: if the doctor discovers a different, unsuspected condition at the time of surgery, I authorize the doctor to perform such other procedures as deemed necessary. I consent to all procedures noted above unless specified as follows: _____

I have been advised that dental devices such as dentures, bridges, caps, crowns, filling and poor dentition are more subject to damage than normal teeth. I agree to accept responsibility for loss or damage to removable teeth if I fail to remove such teeth.

I consent to the photography, videotaping, televising or direct observation of the operations or procedures showing portions of my body, for medical, scientific or educational purposes, provided my identity is not revealed.

Nature, purpose, alternatives: the nature, purpose and consequences of each operation or procedure as well as significant risks involved, possible complications, possible alternative methods of treatment and the likely results of no treatment has been explained to me. I understand that no guarantee or assurance has been made as to the results of the operation or procedure and that it may not cure my condition.

I have been allowed to ask questions about the operation or procedure. In addition, I have read this form or it has been explained to me. I understand the risks and voluntarily consent to the procedure.

MD
Witness (Professional Designation)   Patient/Surrogate/Parent or Guardian

6-5-99   10:30
Date   Time   Relationship to Patient

6-5-99   10:50
Date   Time   Second Witness for Phone/Verbal Consent

46

After obtaining the telephone consent, the doctor did call me, as you can see by the following hospital notes. Dr. # 2 wrote in the hospital notes that he obtained consent from someone other than the patient's wife. He then writes, "Also talked to patient's wife," as though I am some kind of an after thought.

When this doctor called me on Saturday afternoon, right before the surgery was scheduled to start, he inform me that he had a signed consent form, then he asked for my consent. I refused to give it to him. He never once asked for the legal papers that were still in my husband's duffle bag. I was so upset at that time, I never even thought about the papers. I thought a doctor was supposed to respect the wishes of a wife. I was foolish enough to think that if I told him no that would mean he could not do the surgery. When I refused to give consent for the surgery, this doctor harassed me like a used-car salesman.

I finally made a mistake of telling him that if he performed any surgery on my husband, he had better make sure it was legal. I truly thought that would stop him from doing the surgery. At that time, I did not know that the law is on the side of the doctor and not on the side of the patient. I guess my statement to the doctor was what prompted him to write such a condescending statement in the medical records. Dr. # 2 wrote, that I gave him permission to get consent from this other person because I am just a SECOND wife. How disgusting, arrogant and condescending can a doctor be? I was married for 16 years, and I was my husband's legal wife. I was not to be considered a second wife for legal purposes, and I would like to know exactly how the doctor got that information. I certainly did not tell him that. It is usually a first wife who points out that a second wife is a second wife. A second wife normally does not mention this, especially not someone, like myself, who is a very strong-willed person. This doctor makes me sound like a willy-nilly nut, and I do resent his writing lies in the medical records. That is the most chauvinistic and degrading statement I have ever seen written by a doctor about a patient's wife. I NEVER gave my consent.

I do not understand why the doctor did not record this phone call. This is a very modern hospital with the latest in technology. This surgery was not an emergency surgery, nor was it a necessary surgery. I would think the hospital would keep better records than they did. The doctor did not record the phone call. The doctor did not write down a phone number for the person he talked to. The doctor did not get any identification for the person he talked to, such as a driver's license number or a social security number. There is no proof that he even talked to this person he claims to have talked to. All he has for verification is the word of a nurse who was one of my husband's caretakers.

I filed a complaint with the Board of Nursing because I did not think a nurse could legally be a witness. The Nursing Board dismissed my complaint on the basis that the nurse had no legal liability as a witness. I understand that to mean that the nurse could not be sued for being a witness, but that still does not mean that the nurse actually heard or witnessed anything. In fact, not incurring liability is not such a good thing. There should be some stipulations as to who can witness a legal document. Should it be a nurse who works for the hospital?

I think a witness should be someone who does not have anything to lose by accepting or declining to be a witness. Another employee, in my opinion, is not a good witness, because this employee could feel intimidated and be coerced into signing as a witness. I know if I were an employee of a hospital and assigned to a patient's care, I would not want to witness any legal documents concerning that patient.

This Dr. # 2 made a very big mistake. He wrote in the medical records that I had requested a specific person to give consent. What this doctor did not know or understand was that this person was the very reason my husband and I went to a lawyer and had documents drawn up naming me as the attorney-in-fact and my brother-in-law as the alternate attorney-in-fact. If I had recommended this doctor talk to anyone else over the telephone, I would have recommended he talk to my brother-in-law. I simply do not believe the doctor talked to anyone because I cannot find anybody who will corroborate the doctor's statement in the medical records.

I had a fax machine next to where I was sitting while I was talking to the doctor. If I had wanted to give consent, I would have faxed a statement to the doctor. Furthermore, if the doctor had wanted to gain a legal consent, he would have asked me to do so. Dr. # 2 never even got identification, such as a driver's license number or a Social Security number from the person he claims to have gotten consent from. If this is an indication of how our healthcare system works in this country, I can tell you that we are in big trouble. This is enough to make anybody think twice before going to a doctor.

This is a copy, from the medical records, of the doctor's statement, where he talks about me as an afterthought and states I gave him permission to get the telephone consent from someone other than myself. I am not sure how legal this is. I think a transfer of consent should be notarized.

	CCS
?-5-91	Pt. to go to theatre for open lung
2.1919	biopsy. Consent obtained from
20mm	Son. Also talked
	to pts wife. Explained reasons why
	agrees but would rather
	have formal consent form
	pts son since she is
	incompt wife. Goals risks
	verbally explained.
	Questions answered (both pts wife)

The name on the consent form was printed and not written. The printing appeared to look the same as the doctor's printing. I questioned the hospital and was told that the name was printed because it was a verbal consent, taken over the telephone. The hospital's legal counsel verified that the consent was verbal and taken via telephone.

The next document shows that the patient was an inpatient, and there was no emergency. To my understanding, that means there was no reason for gaining consent over the telephone. I spoke with a lawyer about this method of gaining consent for an inpatient surgery, and he would not commit himself to a definite answer. He did say that the hospital might want to rethink their policy of allowing inpatient surgery consents to be taken over the telephone. This led me to believe that this consent might be considered questionable.

Intraoperative Patient Care

Number (above) and Name

Date of Surgery 6/5/99		Emergency ☐	Inpatient ☑	Outpatient ☐	Trauma ☐
Intraoperative Teaching	Done ☐	Verbalizes Understanding ☐	Questions Answered ☐		
Preoperative Assessment Reviewed:		Remains unchanged ☐	Other ☐		
Nursing Notes:	Operative Site Confirmed with Patient ☐	Right ☐	Left ☐	Bilateral ☐	
Allergies: List, ∅					

Comments: Pt intubated (gr) induction on table. Transported to OR via _____
with OR team, & and monitor _____

Nursing Diagnosis #1: Potential for anxiety related to surgical intervention. Goal: Demonstrates decreased anxiety. Plan and Implementation:

Give Clear, Concise explanations. ☑	Convey caring, supportive attitude ☑
Communicate patient concerns to team members ☑	Remain with patient during Induction ☑
Other ☐	

Outcome Nursing Diagnosis #1: Demonstrated adaptive coping strategies. Yes ☑ No ☐
Comments:

Anesthesia	General ☑	Spinal/Epidural ☐	Regional ☐	MAC ☐	RN IV Sed ☐	Local ☐
OR Room # 7		Laminar Flow On ☐		Wound Class: I ☐ II ☐ III ☐ IV ☑		
Pt in Room 12 30	Surgery Start 12 50	Surgery End 13 30	Patient Out Of Room 13 56			

Circulating Nurses	In/Out	In/Out	In/Out	Scrub Personnel	In/Out	In/Out	In/Out
_____ , RN				M. JANASZ, ST.			
Additional Personnel				Additional Personnel			

Consultant 1 DR. _____	Consultant 2
Asst. Consultant 1	Asst. Consultant 2
Fellow/Resident	Fellow/Resident
Other	Other
Anesthesiologist 1 DR. _____	CRNA 1 M. Tiede, CRN
Anesthesiologist 2	CRNA 2
RNFA/PA	RNFA/PA

Procedure Performed: LEFT THORACOTOMY WITH WEDGE BIOPSY LEFT UPPER AND
LEFT LOWER LOBES.

Chapter Six

Next is the terrible job that was done during surgery. First, the anesthesiologist should have objected to giving anesthesia to a man in respiratory failure. I did a lot of reading about anesthesiologists, and I found out that they have the most risky job, because many patients die from the anesthesia and not from the surgery. I do not see how it can be advisable to take a patient, who is in respiratory failure, and put him through a surgery that is not an emergency surgery. This does not make sense to me, unless there was something about the lung tissue that the doctors thought was so valuable.

The surgeon was a contract surgeon who did not work for the hospital and who had numerous malpractice complaints filed against him at that time. The medical board showed eight registered complaints, three of those being cases that were lost in court. I cannot imagine that a doctor with that many complaints should even be working.

I discovered why he still had a medical license. When I investigated the members of the board of medical examiners, I found out that that even the president of the medical board had complaints lodged against him and one case he had lost in court. Other members of the medical board also had complaints lodged against them. I realized at that point that the idea of having a medical board is ridiculous. How can doctors be expected to govern other doctors? Medical boards need to be independent of doctors and of state control. It is my opinion that state-run medical boards are very bad business.

In my opinion, this contract surgeon hacked my husband to death. I read the surgery report, and once surgery started, my husband went into pulmonary arrest, had to have a transfusion, was kept on life support, and was pronounced dead three days later. I just did not understand why this surgery was so important to the doctors. I have done research, and I think the doctors thought my husband had some rare disease, such as the bird flu from China. The one thing I don't understand is that they never contacted the Centers for Disease Control. There is something very suspicious and very peculiar about this entire situation. It appeared to me that the doctors were desperate to operate on my husband and get the lung tissue, but they did not bring in any government agency. I thought maybe it was to benefit this hospital for research. I have only opinions and questions. I have never been able to figure out why this surgery had to be done at all. Following is a copy of the surgery report. It shows that my husband was too ill to live through a surgery.

OPERATIVE REPORT   ORIGINAL SURGICAL RECORD –

5-807-997-1 634510   61   M   (1999)

Green, Mr. William P.   Henderson NV

                PROGRESSIVE, BILATERAL PULMONARY INTERSTITIAL
                INFILTRATES, LEFT BEING WORSE.
                LEFT THORACOTOMY WITH WEDGE RESECTIONS OF THE LEFT
                UPPER AND LEFT LOWER PULMONARY LOBES.
                PROGRESSIVE, BILATERAL PULMONARY INTERSTITIAL
                INFILTRATES, LEFT BEING WORSE.

                SC_MH_02_MOHSUR
06/05/99-2   Surg:  CS

                Progressive, bilateral pulmonary interstitial
                infiltrates, left being worse.
              > Left thoracotomy with wedge resections of the left
                upper and left lower pulmonary lobes.

REQUESTING MAYO PHYSICIAN: ███████████ M.D.

ANESTHESIOLOGIST: ███████████ M.D.

OPERATIVE FINDINGS: The patient had no more than the usual amount of
pleural fluid in the left hemithorax. The lung itself was quite adherent
to the anterior chest, and very, very granular and very hard. The
stapling device almost fractured the lung, and there was a significant air
leak present and expected. The biopsies of both the upper and lower lobes
were submitted for all the cultures and the appropriate analyses.

DESCRIPTION OF PROCEDURE: After the induction of a general anesthetic,
the patient, being in the supine position, was propped with a rolled towel
underneath the left flank. The chest and abdomen were then prepared with
Betadine and alcohol and draped in a sterile manner. An anterior
thoracotomy incision was made and the chest was entered through the
superior aspect of the fifth rib. After appropriate retraction, the wedge
biopsies were obtained with the TA 60 stapling device, and hemostasis was
secured. A single 28-French chest tube was then introduced through a
separate stab incision and secured to the skin with silk. The ribs were
reapproximated with heavy figure-of-eight Vicryls and the rest of the
incision was closed anatomically with absorbable suture. Sterile
dressings were applied, and the patient transferred directly to ICU in
critical condition, but with stable vital signs.

TR: mtr
D&T: 06/05/1999

cc: ███████████ M.D.
     ███████████, M.D.

Recently I checked with the State Board of Medical Examiners to see how many recent complaints had been made against the contract doctor. There were several new complaints and some more cases lost in court. I found out that all the state medical boards belong to a Federal Board of Medical Examiners, so I paid for a report on this doctor from the federal board. The report stated that the doctor had a CLEAN record. That made it very clear to me that the states can protect the reputations and malpractice records of their doctors simply by not turning over to the Federal Board of Medical Examiners records of complaints and of court cases within the state.

I now understand how doctors keep the public from finding out about their malpractice records. This is wrong and dangerous. I also looked into workplace privacy laws, and I found out that doctors have even more protection. If a complaint is filed against a doctor for medical malpractice, the nature of the complaint cannot be disclosed. If it is disclosed, it is a violation of privacy laws.

That does not make sense to me. Doctors work with life and death every day, and what they do is considered private from the very people they treat. Then the state can withhold their complaints from the Federal Medical Board. I cannot be sure I will ever trust a doctor again. Everything they do seems to be private and off-limits to their patients. A person can run a background check on an employee, but that person cannot find out if the doctor they are about to see has complaints filed against him or her. Something is very wrong in America.

We have Better Business Bureaus (BBB) in every state that take complaints on businesses, whether or not they are members of the BBB. The Federal Trade Commission can take complaints on businesses. The nature of these complaints can be revealed, but the names of the people filing these complaints cannot be revealed. What makes doctors different? Why can an agency be sued for compiling a database of complaints filed against doctors. This is a big question, and this is why I do not have a lot of faith in the medical profession. If the BBB can take complaints filed against a plumber, why can't they take complaints filed against a doctor?

This proves that we definitely need a change in the law. Doctors should be governed at the federal level, and the state medical boards should no longer have the opportunity to hide doctors' malpractice complaints. We also need a federal database of doctors with a three strikes, you're out policy on cases lost in court. That way, doctors would not have to worry about the high cost of medical malpractice insurance.

When you read this surgical report and see how the surgery was performed, you can tell that this doctor definitely is not an expert. Otherwise, he would not have so many complaints lodged against him. You can also see that my husband was so ill that he should not have been in surgery.

Chapter Seven

The next part of the story involves the pathologist who did the surgical pathology report on the lung tissue that was taken from my husband during surgery. I could not believe it when I saw the name. I am going to call him Dr. # 3, but it was the same doctor who did the consultation on my husband's case before my husband left the other hospital. I searched all the medical records, but there was no mention by this doctor that he had previously worked on this case as a consultant, and that should have been noted in the medical records. Now I had to wonder why Dr. # 3 was the one doing the report from the surgery.

I had a bad feeling then, and I still have the same bad feeling. I think this doctors either did not know what my husband had or thought it was something rare and important. I will always wonder if this doctor had planned to do research and write journal articles to further his career at the expense of my husband's life. Granted, my husband would have died anyway, but most likely, just not at that time. In addition, I might have had the benefit of being at his side when he died. It is my opinion that these doctors deliberately robbed me of precious last minutes I could have spent with my husband. I really felt that Dr. # 3 wanted this case to study and was not interested in saving my husband's life. So far, I have not found anything in the medical records to keep me from believing this.

Following is the pathology report filed by Dr. # 3. I also noticed a different name listed as the surgeon on this report. The name that was listed was the head of the thoracic department, the doctor who was consulted about the surgery, and the same doctor who did not write any reasons in the medical records about why my husband should have this surgery. That situation leads me to believe that the head of the thoracic department was originally supposed to do this surgery. It is my opinion that he called in the contract surgeon to take his place, probably because he did not want to be involved in this surgery. There has to be some logical reason for bringing in a doctor who had so many malpractice complaints.

We Have the Power

SURGICAL PATHOLOGY BIOPSY REPORT
MAYO HOSPITAL

UNIC NUMBER: 5 807 997 —1 634510 PROCEDURE DATE: 06/05/99
NAME: GREEN,WILLIAM P. REQUESTING PHYSICIAN:
SEX: M AGE: 61 SURGEON:
FROZEN: N REPORT DATE: 06/07/99
ACCESSION #: PS99-2226 HISTORY LOCATION: 2 WEST MCH

SPECIMEN:
Part A: LEFT UPPER LOBE
Part B: LEFT LOWER LOBE

GROSS:
A. Submitted fresh is a wedge shaped fragment of lung tissue measuring 4 x 3 x 1 cm in greatest dimensions. The specimen is pink tan in color and appears somewhat indurated with small 1 mm nodularities noted on cut surface. The specimen is otherwise unremarkable. The specimen is carefully sectioned and submitted in ten (10) cassettes labeled A1-A10 with the first two cassettes (A1-A2) submitted for rapid processing and reading.

B. Submitted fresh is a wedge biopsy of lung labeled left lower lobe. The fragment of tissue measures 2 x 1 x 0.7 cm in maximum dimensions. Upon inspection this tissue is similar to that described above. The color is pink tan. The parenchyma is somewhat indurated and an occasional 1 mm nodule which is whitish in color is noted. The specimen is submitted in two cassettes labeled B1-B2 with cassette B1 submitted for rapid processing.
PS99-2226 A1, A2, A3, A4, A5, A6, A7, A8, A9, A10, B1, B2

DIAGNOSIS:
A,B. OPEN LUNG BIOPSY: Showing necrotizing granulomatous pneumonia with acid fast organisms (see comment).

COMMENT: Both biopsies show an acute necrotizing granulomatous pneumonia with more extensive necrosis in the upper lobes. Some of the airways show mucostasis suggesting there may be a mild underlying component of airway disease and that can be correlated with the clinical and radiologic findings. The major change is a necrotizing granulomatous inflammation associated with surrounding and nonspecific changes of acute lung injury. Within the granulomas acid fast bacilli are identified. GMS stains for fungi are negative. GRAM stains are negative.

Given the history of a prior positive sputum for mycobacterium avium intracellulare, that organism would be favored although other acid fast bacilli could cause this pattern. There does not appear to be significant underlying evidence of dust exposure, particularly silica/silicates.

Report Electronically Signed Out **

PATHOLOGIST/tvc

61

The doctors had no need to talk to me before the surgery, but when my husband was legally dead, they found my number in a hurry. They needed me to sign for him to be taken off life support. Up until that time, the nurses were giving me progress reports that my husband was doing better or doing about the same. The day they needed him taken off life support, I was told that my husband had taken a turn for the worse. It was all lies up until that point. I have the medical records, and I can read. My husband was NEVER getting well in that hospital. He was marked for death from the moment he was accepted at that hospital. He never had one doctor that would care for him. He was passed around like a piece of meat. The best advice I can give anybody is not to go into the hospital unless you have a lawyer to advise you at all times. I just do not know what to think any more. How can doctors and hospitals be so mixed up and confused, and why do we have to pay the ultimate price for it? This question has remained unanswered for far too long.

Dr. # 2 wrote a false statement in the medical records when he stated that I wanted to have someone else give surgical consent. I never wanted anyone interfering in my business. After my husband died, I was alone, and I planned his funeral by myself. Not one person helped me with the arrangements. I made arrangements with Nellis Air Force Base for a military funeral because my husband had been in the Air Force. I chose the casket and the flowers. I arranged for the priest to have graveside services. I went through a lot with the doctors, and if I had been as weak as Dr. # 2 portrayed me to be, I could never have done what I did with planning the funeral.

When it was all over, I bought all the medical records, read all of them, put all the pieces together, contacted personal injury attorneys and filed complaints with the state medical board. That led to even more heartbreak for me. I learned exactly what went on in that hospital, and I was just about to see a huge cover up by using state laws to violate my constitutional rights to due process.

My next decision was to start contacting lawyers. I contacted more than one hundred lawyers, and most of them told me I did not have a case. I was amazed that so much confusion that resulted in a patient's death could go on in a hospital, and I had no recourse. I always questioned the lawyers, and some of them told me that I did not have a case because my husband's illness was terminal and he was going to die anyway. I started wondering why my husband had been transferred on an ambulance plane if he was already going to die. I had not understood prior to that time the seriousness of respiratory failure. In addition, the doctor never specifically told me that my husband was in respiratory failure.

I am an intelligent person, and I can read and understand the facts surrounding my husband's death. At the time he was ill, all the doctor told me was he could get well, or he could die. Now, that is a vague statement for a doctor to make. All I could ascertain from the doctor's statement was that some other hospital might be able to give my husband more help than the one he was in. No doctor ever, at any time, ever told me my husband was going to die. I had to wonder how a lawyer could look at the medical records and know my husband was never going to get well. This is a serious issue, because these doctors were not being honest with me, and I had to find out why. That was when I made a decision to contact the state medical board.

That decision was also an enlightening one. At the time I filed the complaint, I had no idea what tight control doctors had over their profession. I got a lesson about the laws and how they favor doctor's rights over the constitutional rights of Americans.

One day, while I was doing my letter writing and research, I received a letter from the hospital telling me the admitting form had never been signed. The letter further stated that the hospital needed a signature in order to bill the insurance company. This was a shock, because now it was not just the surgery form that did not have an actual signature on it, but it was the admitting form. I could not understand how any hospital could treat a patient without getting any signatures on any of the forms.

This is a copy of the letter the hospital sent:

We Have the Power

March 29, 2000

Mr. William P. Green
762 Butternut Court
Henderson , NV. 89014

We are pleased to continue to provide your Healthcare services at Mayo Clinic Scottsdale.
Recently a request for verification of information and more importantly your signature authorizing us to
release information was mailed to you. **Your insurance claim cannot be filed for reimbursement until the
enclosed form is received with your signature.** If we have no response to our second request, your account
will be updated to a 'self pay' status and a statement for payment in full will be mailed to you.

Please revise any incorrect information on the form, sign it, and return it to us in the enclosed envelope.
EVEN IF YOU MAKE NO CHANGES, PLEASE SIGN AND RETURN THE FORM. Below is a check list
to aid you in review of the form:

PATIENT DEMOGRAPHIC INFORMATION
*   Please verify the address, phone number, security number, date of birth, marital status and gender have all
    been entered correctly. Please also verify or add employer information if applicable.

GUARANTOR DEMOGRAPHIC INFORMATION
*   Please verify the address, phone number, security number, date of birth, and gender have all been entered
    correctly. Please also verify or add employer information if applicable.
*   If the patient is not the account guarantor, please include the relationship of the guarantor to the patient.

SECONDARY ADDRESS
NEXT OF KIN
CONTACT ADDRES

FIRST/SECOND/THIRD INSURANCE
*   Please make a photocopy of the front and back of your insurance cards and return them to us in the
    enclosed envelope along with the signed *Patient Registration Information Form.* Indicate which
    insurance is your primary coverage if you are covered by more than one insurance plan.

SIGNATURE
*   Sign and date the *"Patient Registration Information Form"*, even if you have not made any changes.

Thank you for taking the time to assist us by providing current information for your Mayo Clinic Scottsdale
registration. If you have recently completed this process please disregard this request.

Sincerely,

Supervisor-Registration
Encl: Envelope
      Registration Form

65

I then found the bill from the hospital showing that the insurance company had already been billed and paid. The letter the hospital sent to me clearly stated that the insurance company could not be billed without a signature, but the insurance company had been billed and the hospital had been paid before I even got the letter. I was wondering how a hospital could get away without getting a signature upon admission. I refused to sign the admitting form, and they continued to send the same letter again and again. This is a copy of the form letter the hospital kept sending.

We Have the Power

STATEMENT OF CHARGES

DATE: 19SEP01

FACILITY:
MAYO CLINIC HOSPITAL

WILLIAM P GREEN
ESTATE OF WILLIAM GREEN
2657 WINDMILL PARKWAY 115
HENDERSON, NV   89014-3384

Services Provided:
From: 4JUN99
To: 8JUN99

Patient:	GREEN, WILLIAM P		Account Number:		634510	
Service Date	**Description Code**	**Rev Code**	**Activity Description**	**Units**	**Payments Adj/Chgs**	
8JUN99	RX2619	250	PANCURONIUM BROMIDE 1MG/ML VIA	001	31.55	
8JUN99	RX2619	250	PANCURONIUM BROMIDE 1MG/ML VIA	001	31.55	
8JUN99	RX2619	250	PANCURONIUM BROMIDE 1MG/ML VIA	001	31.55	
8JUN99	RX2823	250	POTASSIUM CHLORIDE 20MEQ/0.1L	005	233.70	
8JUN99	RX2949	250	PROPOFOL 10MG/ML VIAL IV 100ML	001	104.25	
8JUN99	RX3025	250	RANITIDINE HCL 25MG/ML VIAL IN	001	31.80	
8JUN99	RX3025	250	RANITIDINE HCL 25MG/ML VIAL IN	001	31.80	
8JUN99	RX3349	248	THEOPHYLLINE ANHYDROUS 80MG/15	003	5.15	
8JUN99	RX3617	248	PHARMACY NO CHARGE ITEM	001	0.00	
8JUN99	RX3617	248	PHARMACY NO CHARGE ITEM	001	0.00	
30SEP99	71	00	PAYMENT--INSURANCE	001	-1,077.06	
30SEP99	71	00	PAYMENT--INSURANCE	001	-65.70	
30SEP99	71	00	PAYMENT--INSURANCE	001	-116.70	
30SEP99	71	00	PAYMENT--INSURANCE	001	-23.80	
5OCT99	71	00	PAYMENT--INSURANCE	001	-81.90	
5OCT99	71	00	PAYMENT--INSURANCE	001	-170.80	
5OCT99	71	00	PAYMENT--INSURANCE	001	-268.10	
5OCT99	71	00	PAYMENT--INSURANCE	001	-268.10	
5OCT99	71	00	PAYMENT--INSURANCE	001	-60.20	
5OCT99	71	00	PAYMENT--INSURANCE	001	-859.60	
5OCT99	71	00	PAYMENT--INSURANCE	001	-23.80	
5OCT99	71	00	PAYMENT--INSURANCE	001	-23.80	
5OCT99	71	00	PAYMENT--INSURANCE	001	-1,960.70	
5OCT99	71	00	PAYMENT--INSURANCE	001	-60.20	
6OCT99	71	00	PAYMENT--INSURANCE	001	-60.20	
15FEB00	71	00	PAYMENT--INSURANCE	001	-27,126.87	
			TOTAL		6,172.00	

I have never had any experiences with hospitals before this, but I do know a lot about business and contract law. A contractor or plumber cannot work on your house without a signed contract to do so. Why would a hospital be able to treat a patient, under conditions that were not emergency conditions, without a signed agreement? I am not a lawyer, and I am not an expert on the law, but I am smart enough to know that there is something wrong in the American healthcare system. Admitting a patient and billing insurance companies without a signature should not be allowed, nor should it be tolerated.

I wrote to the insurance company. I was sure they would be upset about paying for a surgery and hospitalization when the hospital had failed to get a signed admission form. I was wrong. I received a letter from the lawyer for the insurance company. He explained in that letter that the insurance policy was an employer-funded policy and the insurance company was only the administrator. It was obvious that nobody was concerned about the money the casino had paid out, even though the hospital admission form had never been signed. Furthermore, the lawyer stated that my case was a medical malpractice case. Now I was really confused. More than a hundred lawyers had refused my husband's case, but this lawyer was now calling it a medical malpractice case. I knew something was very wrong. Following is a copy of the letter from the attorney representing the insurance company.

HINSHAW & CULBERTSON

APPLETON, WISCONSIN
BELLEVILLE, ILLINOIS
BROOKFIELD, WISCONSIN
CHAMPAIGN, ILLINOIS
CHICAGO, ILLINOIS
CRYSTAL LAKE, ILLINOIS
FT. LAUDERDALE, FLORIDA
JACKSONVILLE, FLORIDA
JOLIET, ILLINOIS
LISLE, ILLINOIS
MIAMI, FLORIDA

PIPER JAFFRAY TOWER
SUITE 3100
222 SOUTH NINTH STREET
MINNEAPOLIS, MINNESOTA 55402

612.333.3434
TELEFAX: 612.334.8888

MILWAUKEE, WISCONSIN
MUNSTER, INDIANA
PEORIA, ILLINOIS
PHOENIX, ARIZONA
ROCKFORD, ILLINOIS
ST. LOUIS, MISSOURI
SAN FRANCISCO, CALIFORNIA
SPRINGFIELD, ILLINOIS
TAMPA, FLORIDA
WAUKEGAN, ILLINOIS

Thomas E. Sanner
Direct: 612.334.2641
SannerT@hinshawmn.com

September 10, 1999

Ms. Joan Green
P.O. Box 50822
Henderson, NV 89016

   Re: Investigation Concerning William Green
     Our File No. 761022

Dear Ms. Green:

  Please be advised that our law firm represents The TPA, Inc. ("The TPA"). I have been asked by The TPA to respond to your letter of August 26, 1999, directed to Mark Davis of The TPA in Phoenix Arizona.

  Let me first say that I am sorry to learn of the death of your husband following his hospitalization at the ▇▇▇▇▇▇▇▇▇▇. You have my sympathy.

  Unfortunately, The TPA is not in a position to conduct an "investigation" as you request in your letter. The TPA is a third-party administrator of self-funded health benefit plans. The TPA does not investigate potential claims of unethical practice or malpractice on the part of healthcare providers. It would appear that your complaints filed with Medical Licensing Board in Arizona would be the appropriate means of further pursuing this matter. I hope you receive some answer to your inquiry.

  Please contact me if you have any questions or comments. Thank you.

      Very truly yours,

      Thomas E. Sanner

TES/jma
c: Mr. Mark Davis

100/22182654 9/10/99   A PARTNERSHIP INCLUDING PROFESSIONAL CORPORATIONS

I called the state insurance commissioners office, fraud division. I figured there must be some type of fraud going on for this to have happened. First, I carefully checked out the four elements of fraud. First, there has to be an intent to defraud the insurance company. I thought the hospital was responsible for getting a signature on the insurance form, and filing a claim without a signature must constitute intent. Second, there must be knowledge that they are doing wrong. Once again, I thought that the fact that the hospital did not get a signature and sent out a form letter stating so, would mean they had knowledge they billed the insurance company without a signature. Third, there must be misrepresentation that would create or assist in creating a false impression that would lead to the claim being paid. I thought the fact that the hospital filed the claim and wrote "signature on file" when there was no signature on file was the same as creating a false impression that led to the payment of the claim. Fourth, there has to be reliance that the insurer would not have paid the claim without the representation. I was certain the insurance company would not have paid the claim without containing the statement "signature on file". I was wrong all four times. The investigator from the insurance commissioner's office informed me that there was no fraud because the services billed for were actually performed. He further told me that the only way you can have fraud is for the hospital to bill for services they have not performed. I did not carry that any further. It became obvious to me that insurance commissioners did not pay much attention to what hospitals do or do not do.

I certainly was not having any luck with getting attorneys, or anyone else, to pay attention to this horrible mess that had surrounded my husband's illness. Every attorney told me that I did not have any kind of case against either the doctors or the hospital. I just had a difficult time accepting this because so many strange things had happened throughout my husband's illness, hospitalization and death. What it all came back to was the Uniform Determination of Death Act (UDDA). My husband was legally dead before he left the hospital in Las Vegas. The doctor should have informed me, but he didn't, and there is no law that says he was supposed to inform me.

After reading the UDDA, I gained a certain understanding of what I was dealing with. This is how it appeared to me. Once a person is old or terminally ill that person becomes useless in society. He or she can no longer work, earn money, spend money, buy stocks, and be part of the economic process. Therefore, this person is rendered useless to society for nothing more than body parts for research or transplant. That is the only economic value to the life of an old or terminally ill person. Basically, nobody is interested anymore, and I was getting that message loud and clear.

This started me thinking about human dignity, and a person's right to die according to his or her own wishes or own faith. I am not talking about assisted suicide or mercy killing. I am simply talking about a person's right to die naturally. My husband and I had an agreement that we would not allow a surgery to be performed on the other person if he or she was already terminally ill. We also had certain spiritual beliefs that we should not be sedated unnecessarily at the end of life. These are just deep personal beliefs. I tried to abide by them for my husband, but I was ignored, and the decisions for my husband's care were taken out of my hands.

I have wondered why elderly and terminally ill people cannot have the same rights as a well person. Why can't a person's value be in human life? Why does everything in America have to be dollars and cents? This argument goes to the heart of what America really is, and how others around the world see the American people. It is possible that we need a change of attitude in this country. We need to start caring once again. We seem to be great with disasters around the world, but what about our own disasters? What about elderly Americans? What about terminally ill Americans? What about homeless Americans? Do we really care? It is time for us to evaluate what is going on in this country.

Business in America has become so greedy. CEO's are paid millions, while retained earnings on the balance sheet can only carry the company a month or two without consumers. The disparity that Howard Dean needs to be talking about is the disparity on the balance sheet. Corporate officers and members of management should not be allowed to collect salaries that are greater than the profits, and there should be laws about a company functioning without enough money in reserve. We, the people, need to start paying attention to what is going on in the corporate world. Healthcare is intermingled with the corporate world, through affiliations with pharmaceutical companies and insurance companies.

We also need to look at nonprofit corporations, such as the hospital my husband was in. This hospital is a subsidiary of a private foundation, and it was operating at a loss. I looked at the Forms 990, and I discovered that the hospital never made a profit. It operated at a loss for two years. Every third year, money was transferred from the fund balance of the parent corporation, a private foundation. This money came from various sources and charities. This made me wonder why health care is so expensive in this country, when we are the ones funding it. It works like this.

When you contribute money to charities such as the United Way, that money is collected and distributed. This hospital was one of the recipients. Patients are treated in this hospital and then insurance pays the bill. Any charges the insurance company does not pay, the patient is liable for. If the patient cannot or does not pay these charges, the hospital has a law firm on a million dollar a year retainer that does the collection work for this hospital. That law firm belongs to a former United States Senator. We need to correct this situation in America so everyone can get medical help. We also need to correct the flaws in the healthcare system so that everyone who needs healthcare can get good healthcare. We are America, and we need to be the best and give the best.

Many people are leaving this country because they do not agree with the policies and laws of America. I do not agree with everything in this country, but I refuse to leave. I truly believe in the average person in America. If we organized, with the right leader, Howard Dean or someone like him, who truly understands the depth of the problems the average citizen faces in this country, we could start making members of the house and the senate accountable to us once again. We could start rewriting and changing laws that would make a difference for generations to come. I am afraid that if these problems are ignored, we are on the road to fascism. That is what happens when corporations gain too much control and power and rule the lives of the citizens.

Chapter Eight

The next issue I decided to work on was the autopsy and the biopsy from the surgery. I wanted to know exactly what my husband died from. All the doctors would say was that he died from COPD. That means chronic obstructive pulmonary disease. It is a one-size-fits-all diagnosis that is used to cover a wide range of pulmonary diseases. That was ridiculous to call that the cause of death. My husband had drug-resistant micobacterium avium intracellular and VRE and severe lung damage, and the doctors were using the all-encompassing term of COPD to state his cause of death. I did not then and will not now accept that.

I wanted the lung tissue from the open lung biopsy to be sent to another doctor who specialized in Silicosis. I made my own transfer form and sent it to the hospital requesting the lung tissue be sent to this other doctor. The hospital did as I requested, but the quantity of lung tissue they had was a shock to me. It appeared the pathologist, Dr. # 4, had removed all the lung tissue from my husband's body. I read the entire autopsy report, but the removal of lung tissue was not listed there.

This bothered me because it goes to accountability. How can a doctor take parts or organs from a deceased person, whether they are for transplant or for research, and not list the removal in the autopsy report? I would never have known the doctors had done this if I had not wanted a second opinion on the biopsy.

I also did not like the way my husband and I were treated, and I really did not feel this hospital had been honest with me. I felt there was no reason they should benefit in any way from my husband's death. Every time I asked question of the doctors that treated my husband, I was referred to another high-priced attorney who was also on a million dollar retainer. I could not understand why these doctors needed an attorney when they claimed they had done nothing wrong. The doctors have never answered my questions, and the attorney has not answered my questions.

This is a copy of the letter from the hospital specifying the quantity of lung tissue.

September 28, 1999

Department of Pathology

RE: William P. Green
MC#: 5-807-997-1
DOB: 9/17/37

Dear Dr.

At the written request of Joan Green, surviving spouse of William P. Green, we are releasing all of Mr. Green's pathology material to you. Specifically, enclosed herewith are:

1. Open lung biopsy – 17 slides and 7 paraffin blocks (PS99-2226;6/5/99)
2. Autopsy lungs - 26 slides and 20 paraffin blocks (AA12-99;6/9/99)
3. Right and left autopsy lungs - wet tissue (AA12-99; 6/9/99)

Mrs. Green requested that we transfer all pathology to your possession. Therefore, all communications and charges incurred regarding your review, storage, or return of the specimens to Mrs. Green should be directed to her at: P.O. Box 50822, Henderson, NV 89016-08221.

Sincerely,

Pathology Secretary

:js

CC Joan Green (via facsimile 888-433-5683)

Enclosures

Sent via Certified Mail

This is where the Uniform Anatomical Gift Act (UAGA) works for the doctors and hospitals. The hospital is allowed to take body parts for research. Even the surgery form grants the hospital permission to keep and use for research all body parts and tissue removed during surgery. This was extremely difficult for me. I had buried my husband, but the hospital kept his lungs without my knowledge. Because of the law, the hospital did not need my consent. The entire situation was becoming more disturbing by the minute, and I was the one who did not have a legal leg to stand on.

I then received a letter from the hospital's attorney. Not only did the attorney inform me that the hospital was releasing the body parts to me, but she also put in writing that the consent for the surgery was definitely a telephone consent. Even with that admission in writing, I still could not get an attorney to take a case against the hospital.

We Have the Power

September 24, 1999

Ms. Joan Green
P.O. Box 50822
Henderson, NV 89016-08221

Re: William P. Green

Dear Ms. Green:

I write to respond to your recent letters to ▮▮▮▮▮ and ▮▮▮▮, M.D. So that we may more readily respond to your inquiries, we ask that you direct all future communications to my attention at ▮▮▮▮▮.

As for your request that we produce medical research, we regret that we simply cannot engage in extensive literature searches for patients and their families. The demands for patient care do not afford us the time to provide this service. However, you are welcome to utilize our patient library, which is located on the concourse level of the ▮▮▮▮.

Concerning consent for Mr. Green's open lung biopsy, the records indicate that ▮▮▮▮, M.D. secured verbal consent on June 5, 1999, from Mr. Green's ▮▮ Because the consent was secured via telephone, it is witnessed, and the name of the individual giving consent is printed. The printed name on the consent form is not intended to be a signature. Dr. ▮▮ also spoke with you before the biopsy about its goals and risks, and you too agreed that it should be done. You also suggested securing consent from Mr. Green's ▮▮ which was done. Finally, the "Durable Power of Attorney for Health Care Decisions" which you attached to your August 17, 1999 letter to Mr. Bour was not provided or mentioned to any of Mr. Green's healthcare providers at Mayo Clinic Hospital during Mr. Green's hospitalization.

Finally, **we will forward all of Mr. Green's available pathology specimens to** ▮▮ **, M.D.,** pursuant to your September 21, 1999, written request to Dr. ▮▮ Specifically, at your request, we will relinquish possession and terminate our role as custodian of Mr. Green's slides, blocks, and wet tissue from the autopsy and open lung biopsy. **Following our release to Dr. ▮▮, your designee, ▮▮ will no longer be responsible for maintenance of Mr. Green's pathology slides, blocks, or tissue.**

Again, if you have any further requests, please direct your inquiry to my attention and I will be happy to assist you. Thank you.

Very truly yours,

Legal Counsel

79

I wrote to the Chair of the Board of Governors of the hospital about the taking of the body parts. I told him that I thought the hospital accepted my husband only for the purposes of obtaining his lung tissue and doing research on his lung tissue. I already knew about the Internal Revenue Code that stipulates patient care must support research and education in order for the hospital to maintain a tax-exempt status. The response from the hospital Chair was surprising. The Chair mentions in his letter that at no time was a desire for research grant money the motivation for the care of my husband. I wonder what the IRS would think about the hospital not wanting to do research, when research is a condition of maintaining their tax-exempt status. I also wonder why the hospital took a legally dead man into their hospital for surgery when they were only motivated for caring for him. A first -year resident would have known that surgery would kill my husband. The chair also referred to the complaint I filed with the medical board. He seemed to being relying heavily on medical board's dismissal. Here is a copy of the letter from the Chair of the Board of Governors.

March 28, 2001

Ms. Joan Green
2657 Windmill Parkway, #115
Henderson, NV 89014-3384

Re: William Green

Dear Ms. Green:

I recently received your March 6, 2001, letter and attachments to Dr. ██████████ As Chairman of the Board of Governors for ██████████████, I take the issues you raised concerning your husband's treatment at ██████████ very seriously. I sincerely regret that you continue to believe your husband was not treated appropriately, notwithstanding findings by the ██████ Board of Medical Examiners and the ████████████ of Nursing supportive of ████ care. Mr. Green was at all times treated consistent with ██████ primary principle of care, "the needs of the patient come first." At no time was a desire for "research grant money" the motivation for the care Mr. Green received. Mr. Green's medical records were not "manipulated," and consent for his surgery was properly secured and documented. After critical analysis of the complaints you raised, we continue to believe that Mr. Green received appropriate evaluation and treatment at Mayo Clinic Hospital.

Sincerely,

██████████████████████

██████████████████
Chair, Board of Governors

MBO/jed

cc: ██████████ M.D.

TNB05216.ltr.L.PT

81

By this time, I was beginning to feel that all doctors thought that anyone who was not a doctor or a lawyer was just plain stupid and had no right questioning their actions. My degree is not in law or medicine, but I am far from stupid. I wanted to complete my entire investigation, even though I knew I did not have a case. My objective was to write this book so that others would understand what is going on in the medical community. Hopefully this book, at the very least, will keep someone else from going through what my husband I went through.

The situation I went through is the very reason I do not believe President Bush about the medical malpractice being caused by frivolous lawsuits. I think Bush's argument is bogus, and I think it is just one more attempt to tie the hands of the American public by not allowing them to sue doctors. After what I went through, I do not see how anybody can get a lawsuit against a doctor. I think a person would have to go in for heart surgery and end up with a leg amputated instead. This would be something visible that could not be overlooked. If that is the case, then the person should have the right to sue. President Bush needs to understand that there are incompetent doctors in the system. Unless the system is restructured, those incompetent doctors will remain in the system. The cure for lowering medical malpractice insurance rates is to get rid of the incompetent doctors, such as the contract surgeon who operated on my husband. Capping lawsuits and further hurting the American people is not the answer. Incompetent doctors do real damage to patients.

President Bush is not in favor of getting bad doctors out of the healthcare system and he is also not in favor of getting new laws written that would insure terminally ill patients would not be killed in hospitals. All Bush wants to do is protect doctors and pharmaceutical companies, so that nothing will interfere with making profits. It does not appear to me that the lives of elderly and terminally ill Americans mean anything to him.

Chapter Nine

The worst was yet to come for me. I had to complete the investigation with the Board of Medical Examiners before I could write this book. While corresponding with the Board, I found progress notes from Dr. #1 to my husband's doctor in Las Vegas, Nevada. Dr. # 1 was the doctor who recommended and ordered the surgery. In those progress notes, Dr. # 1 actually covers up the fact that he ordered surgery by never mentioning the surgery. Dr. # 1 lied and said my husband was continued on the management plan that had been initiated at the hospital in Las Vegas. My husband was not continued on the management plan, because he was not in the hospital for more than 12 hours before he was hacked up in surgery and placed on life support.

Furthermore, I do not understand how Dr. # 1 can comment on what caused my husband's death. He does not know anything. I requested the lung tissue be sent to another pathologist. Suddenly that doctor did not want to make any comments on my husband's death. I am the one who eventually ended up with the lung tissue, and I sought the help of a pathologist who is very knowledge in the area of industrial disease. He is in Canada, and I feel his knowledge is far superior to any doctor I have talked to in the United Sates.

PROGRESS NOTE

RE: WILLIAM P. GREEN

DATE: June 17, 1999

I received a call from Dr. ████████████s at the ██████████ in ████████, ████████████s informed me that Mr. Green had expired. I told him that Mrs. Green had given me the bad news.

Apparently, Mr. Green had an autopsy. It was discovered that his lung disease was underlying emphysema, and all of the lung abnormalities that had been seen on CT scan could be attributable to acute granulomatous pneumonia from mycobacterial disease. There was also extensive airway inflammation from the adult respiratory distress syndrome.

They essentially continued the management plan that we had initiated at ████████ Hospital. I informed him that a consultation from the National Jewish Medical and Research Center also approved the therapy.

████████████, M.D

JJW:pmss-s

After reading this progress report, I lost all respect for doctors and everyone in the entire medical profession. There are no ethics left. I value my life too much to even go to a doctor for anything, unless I feel I am dying. Then if they kill me, I guess it will not matter if I am dying anyway. I have my spiritual beliefs, and do not want any doctor doing surgery or anything else that is against my wishes. I take natural remedies to keep my immune system strong, and I work to stay healthy and avoid any type of medical treatment.

I had some problems around the time of my husband's death and for a few years before. My hair and fingernails had always been strong and grew fast. I noticed for about the last five years before my husband passed away that my hair and nails were breaking all the time. I finally started getting one infection after the other throughout my body, and it seemed I was forever taking antibiotics. I now think my hair and fingernails were weakened because of the infections in his body. I searched for natural remedies and found BIOZAMAS. They are all natural, and I purchase off the Internet at www.allnaturalantioxidants.com. I finally have my health back. My hair is growing again and my fingernails, too. I do not have any more problems with infected teeth or any other kind of infection. Between the BIOZAMAS and the Melaluca products I seem to be getting better every day.

I had filed complaints with the state medical board on Drs. #1, #2, # 3 and # 4 and the issues I have gone over so far. Now, I will show how the medical board handled these complaints and how the state laws kept me from ever finding out what happened regarding the hospitalization and the surgery. I filed complaints on the actions of all four doctors, but the board only recognized the actions of one doctor, and that was Dr. # 2, the doctor who obtained consent for the surgery. I had to re-file additional complaints against doctors # 1, # 3, and # 4.

The medical board dismissed the charges against Dr. #2. I was allowed five minutes to speak about what happened. The doctors, in a private hearing with the investigator, dismissed the case. The doctors based the dismissal on the fact that the investigator had given them proof that the doctor had properly secured the consent for surgery. One doctor made the motion, and another public board member seconded the motion. I read the bio on the second board member, and this member's background did not include any work history or education in the areas of law or medicine. I did not think this person was qualified to make a judgment on this case. It was also interesting to note that on this same day another case against another doctor had been dismissed. It was a case filed by someone other than myself, and it was filed against the doctor who was the contract surgeon in my case.

State Board of Medical Examiners

Assistant Director, Licensing/Operations

Telephone (602) 874-2700 • Fax (602) 255-1848 • In State Toll Free (877) 255-2212

February 7, 2000

Ms. Joan Green
P.O. Box 50822
Henderson, NV 89016

Dr.#2

RE: J.G. (Pt. ▮▮▮) vs. ▮▮▮▮▮, M.D. (Inv. # ▮▮▮)

Dear Ms. Green:

The ▮▮▮▮ Board of Medical Examiners considered the above-referenced matter during the course of the February 2000 Regular meeting.

Following a complete and thorough review of all pertinent and available information, the Board concluded in Open Session that the doctor was not in violation of the Medical Practice Act of the State of ▮▮▮▮ and, accordingly, dismissed the matter.

On behalf of the Board of Medical Examiners, thank you for allowing the Board to review this matter. Should you have any questions, please contact ▮▮▮▮▮▮▮ Coordinator, at ▮▮▮▮▮▮

Respectfully,

▮▮▮▮▮▮▮

Board Operations Administrator

GM/lkm

Cc: Investigative File
        License File
        ▮▮▮▮ M.D.

Americans with Disabilities Act: Persons with disabilities may request reasonable accommodations by contacting the Board of Medical Examiners ▮▮▮▮ ▮▮▮▮▮▮▮▮▮ uests should be made as early as possible to allow time to arrange the accommodation.

When the board members dismiss a case, they claim to have "adjudicated" the case. I found this very interesting because adjudication is the determination of issues in a lawsuit. It is a judgment of a court settling matters finally. What this means to me is that the medical board is assuming the role of a court of law. I really do not think this is legal. There are no members on the medical board that are licensed to practice law, so I find the use of the word "adjudicated" questionable.

I asked the board to substantiate with case law or with documentation, how they arrived at their decision to dismiss charges. I felt that was reasonable, since I was the claimant in the issue. They refused.

I honestly felt that a telephone consent was not proper for a non-emergency surgery. I also felt that not getting additional information, such as a driver's license number or Social Security Number, was wrong. Furthermore, I felt that writing false statements in the medical records was wrong. I had not agreed to the surgery, and the doctor had no proof that I did. He also lied when he wrote a fictitious statement in the medical records and had a nurse at the hospital witness it. I also could not find anybody who could corroborate the doctor's story. I really thought the Board of Medical Examiners would listen to me, but they did not. They sent me a letter stating that the charges against the doctor had been dismissed.

I wrote to the Board requesting supporting documentation and the information acquired during the investigation that was used to exonerate these doctors. I truly wanted to see what proof the medical board had that exonerated the doctor. I was not only denied the proof, but I was denied case law that would substantiate of the dismissal. I was told that information was private and could not be given out.

Now I knew something was very wrong. I live in America, where we are free. There are no legal decisions that can be kept from us. Doing what this board did means that the board of medical examiners, with the ability to adjudicate a case, is really a kangaroo court. It is an unauthorized court that claims to have legal authority, but does not have any legal authority and takes the law into its own hands. I knew that if the law protected this medical board or court, that state law was violating my 14th amendment federal constitutional rights, so I continued my research to get to the bottom of this matter.

The response I received stated that Title 32, Chapter 13, Section 32-1451 specifically gives the Board authority to dismiss a case. In addition I was told the doctor did not violate the Medical Practice Act. There were two separate issues that I had to research.

First I read the law, and it stated that the "public" could not get information from the Board. I then wrote again telling the board members that I was not the "public." I told them I was the claimant. To my surprise, I received this letter telling me that it is the ruling of the attorney general that everybody is considered to be the "public." The claimant is part of the public and is treated as the "public."

I wondered why they did not want anyone to get information regarding board investigations, even the people who filed the complaints and already had access to the medical records. I know medical records are private, but the information I was looking for was not in the medical records. I already had the medical records. They are legally my personal property, and I can put them on a billboard if I choose to do so. All I wanted was documentation or case law to substantiate the doctor's dismissal. This is the letter the medical board sent to me.

June 28, 2001

Joan Green
P.O. Box 60822
Henderson NV 89016

Re: Joan Green v. ██████████ M.D. (Inv. #██████)

Dear Ms. Green:

Your letter of June 8, 2001, asks for the authority under which the Board declines to release information from its investigative files. The authority is A.R.S. § 32-1451.01(C), which provides that "...records or reports kept by the board as a result of the investigation procedure outlined in this chapter are not available to the public." This has been interpreted by the Arizona Attorney General to include the complainant and/or the family of the complainant. The Board, therefore, in compliance with state law, does not release information from its investigative files.

Sincerely,

██████████

T██████████
Deputy Director

TA/rsg

cc: ██████████ Executive Director
      File

I was curious about the Medical Practice Act. I went to the law library and nobody there even knew what it was. I called the medical board to ask them what it was, and even the board employees could not clearly define it. The best information I could get was that it is part of Title 32, Chapter 13 of the state law. I went online and found the state law, and chapter has to do with the following: Board of Medical Examiners, Licensing, Regulation, Emergency Aid, Transfusions, Dispensing of Drugs and devices. After reading this, I realized that the medical board had played a very unethical legal trick on me and probably on a lot of other people.

I filed a complaint of medical malpractice, but the scope of the board does not cover malpractice, so the board then dismisses the case stating there is no violation of the Medical practice Act. Because the Medical Practice Act is vague and not clearly defined, there is no way to dispute the word of the medical board. I realized it was a way for the board to get rid of me, to make me shut up and go away. I did not, and I will not.

I was so angry with the Board for not listening to me and for only filing charges against the one doctor, that I wrote a separate complaint against the other three doctors. I specifically mentioned that Dr. # 1 did not have a proper medical history when requesting surgery, that Dr. # 1 made a poor choice in requesting a surgery that would obviously kill the patient, that Dr. # 1 did not tell the truth to the patient's primary physician in Nevada, and that Dr. # 1 did not properly document the surgery consultation. I mentioned that Dr. # 3 did not document in the autopsy report the total amount of lung tissue taken from the patient. I mentioned that Dr. # 4 did not mention in the medical records his prior involvement in the patient case when he consulted on it.

I already knew what kind of an answer I would get, but I had to have it documented. This is a copy of it. The Executive Director of the Board dismissed the charges against the doctors by Executive order. She claimed to have run an "exhaustive" investigation, but she did not have to disclose any of the information collected during the investigation nor did she have to support the dismissal with case law. There is no way a private citizen can win against a doctor. They have more protection that the mafia ever had.

We Have the Power

State Board of Medical Examiners

November 9, 2001

Mrs. Joan Green

Dr. #4   Dr. #1

RE: J.G. (Patient William Green) v. ███████, M.D., ████████
M.D., and ████████, M.D., Case #MD-████
Dr. #3

Dear Mrs. Green:

On May 14, 2001 the ███████ Board of Medical Examiners (Board) initiated an investigation based on the allegations set forth in your complaint against Drs. ███████, and ███ that involved the care and treatment of your husband, William Green. You cited numerous quality of care issues involving these physicians that included Dr. ███████ failure to mention his consultation on the patient's condition prior to his admission to ███████████ Dr. ███████ failure to obtain a prior medical history on the patient, his failure to properly diagnose the patient, his poor decision regarding the necessity of the patient's surgery and the likelihood of the patient's survival, his misrepresentation of the patient's medical condition to the patient's ████████████, his failure to document the thoracic surgery consult, and his diagnosis and treatment of the patient prior to completion of the necessary hospital admission and financial responsibility forms. Lastly, you cited Dr. Leslie for his failure to adequately account for tissue samples taken from your husband during the post mortem examination and his failure to return those samples to the patient's remains prior to his release to the mortuary.

An exhaustive investigation by Board medical investigators and a staff medical consultant concluded that each of the named physicians met the community standard of care. Each of the physicians provided a detailed response to the allegations and the well-documented medical records reviewed by the Board medical consultant substantiated their accounts of the incidents. The medical care provided by each of these practitioners was appropriate and in concert with acceptable medical standards.

Therefore, due to the lack of substantive evidence to sustain violations of the Medical Practices Act, your complaint is being dismissed pursuant to the Executive Director's delegated authority under A.R.S. § 32-1405(C)(21). If there is new evidence that was not submitted during the initial investigation, you may appeal this action to the Board.

Thank you for permitting the Board to review this matter.

Sincerely,

Executive Director

Chapter Ten

I was told that the attorney general interpreted the law in a manner that the claimant was the public. I wanted to know how this could be. I went to the law library again to find out about interpretations of the law by the attorney general. I was told that they would be on the attorney general's website. I went to the website, but the interpretation of the law I was looking for was not there. I went back to the law library, and that was when I found the case law that caused this entire problem. I located the case number and bought the case. That case seemed to be the only thing so far that was public record. I went to West Law on the Internet and purchased the case. Here it is, the case that caused me so much grief.

Court of Appeals of Arizona,
Division 1, Department C.

ARIZONA BOARD OF MEDICAL EXAMINERS, Petitioner,

v.

The SUPERIOR COURT of Arizona In and For MARICOPA COUNTY,
the Honorable
Lawrence O. Anderson, a judge thereof, Respondents,

Eveline Maria MOOS and Richard W. Moos, husband and wife, Real Parties in
Interest.

No. 1 CA-SA 96-0158.

Aug. 20, 1996.

After reading the case, I discovered that one doctor, Dr. Richard Moos, was the cause of all the problems I had endured with the doctors and the members of the medical board. These problems were created when Dr. Moos' wife wanted to divorce him and Dr. Moos did not want to comply with a subpoena in his divorce case. This subpoena was for psychologist's records that were gathered during the course of the medical board's examination where psychologist-client privilege did not apply to the relationship between the psychologist and the physician. The court ordered the records to be turned over in discovery. Grant Woods, the Attorney General at that time, filed a motion of special action challenging the order entered in the Superior Court, which ordered the psychologist to comply with a subpoena. The trial court order was then reversed, and the records did not have to be turned over to the court by the board of medical examiners..

Now, thanks to Dr. Moos and Attorney General Grant Woods, I cannot even find out how or why the Board of Medical examiners dismissed cases against four doctors. All I wanted to know was what kind of proof the board found in their investigation that would prove that the doctor followed proper procedure for gaining surgical consent.

To give me this information would not compromise any medical records of any person. It certainly would not compromise my husband's medical records because I have them. I legally have possession of his medical records, so that is not an issue. What is an issue is that I believe the Board of Medical Examiners is violating my 14th Amendment Rights to due process under the law and possibly the rights of numerous other citizens who have been denied the same information I have been denied. In addition, if they Board has exonerated the doctors and does not have proof other than the word of the doctors, the Board might be concealing a crime or obstructing justice. These are very important issues, and the lives of American citizens are at stake.

I think Grant Woods should publicly explain his reasons for protecting the records of Dr. Richard Moos. While writing this book, I looked up the medical records of Dr. Moos, and I discovered that the medical board now has one open case against Dr. Moos and one case resulting in payment in court. I think those are a lot of charges considering the board will not give out information on a case once the board has dismissed it. Once dismissed, a complaint against a doctor disappears forever.

President Bush could not find a frivolous lawsuit to compare to this flagrant disregard for justice in America. I want Grant Wood to explain his actions, and I want the medical board to reopen every case since this ruling in 1996. I am told I live in a free society, and I want my rights respected. I still want the information I requested from the medical board, and I intend to get it.

I tried to get the media involved in this issue, but they simply were not interested. I am not sure if the media is more interested in our rights or ratings. From where I stand, it does not appear that the media is willing to go against doctors and an attorney general. One reporter at the local newspaper told me that there was not a story regarding what happened to me. This reporter said, "It's the law. I think it's a bad law, but it's the law. If you don't like it, why don't you change it". That is another reason I continued to research the law. Now I know that it is more than a bad law. I think I have proof that it is an illegal law. It is in the US Constitution that states cannot write laws or interpret laws in any manner that violates our constitutional rights. I believe this law does. The Board of Medical Examiners must provide me, the claimant, with proof that substantiates their dismissal of my complaint. The board claims that this material cannot be subpoenaed into another court case. That is ludicrous. If I were trying to get information on another person's medical records, I could understand the denial. I am trying to get information on my husband's case, and I am his legal representative. Furthermore, denying me this information could result in a criminal action of covering up a crime. I want to know just exactly who gave consent for my husband's surgery.

I went to the American Trial Lawyer's Association (ATLA), and they told me they know all about these laws and the laws are the same in every state. When I asked what they were going to do about them, I was told they do not have enough resources to do anything. This left me wondering whose side ATLA is really on.

I have a website, www.JoanLGreen.com. I am petitioning for an examination of how state medical boards operate and what are the criteria for dismissing cases. I am also petitioning for an investigation of the National Law Commissioners. They need to be aware that the uniform state laws they write and promote are causing violations of constitutional rights. If you are interested and want to sign the petition, please visit my website.

I have previously written to several United States Senators regarding this matter. First I wrote to Senators John Ensign and Harry Reid, because they are my senators in Nevada. I waited for several months and never got a response. This made me think they just did not want to become involved because groups of medical professionals contribute to their campaigns. Then I wrote to Senators John McCain and John Kyl, because they are in the state where the medical board and the hospital are. I thought Senator McCain would be interested because he says the system is broken and needs to be fixed. He did respond, but he never acknowledged the content of my letter. Senator McCain just thanked me for keeping him apprised of what goes on in his district. Senator Kyl never responded to my letter.

Senators do not have to respond to anyone who is not a resident of their state. I just thought that I would get a response because this is such a large problem and does involve facilities in their state. My last hope was to write to the two senators who claim to be interested in health care issues, Senators Clinton and Kennedy. There was no response from them either.

We need to have elected officials who will truly represent us, and we can make them accountable to us. We also need to have laws that work for us and do not restrict our rights, especially our right to due process. If people do not stand up for their rights now, there will not be any rights left for future generations. This is an issue that each and every one of us must ponder. If we want a democracy, then we are the ones who have to make it work. It will take our sweat. There is no way we can pay anybody else to do the job for us. We, the people can do this, and we can do it peacefully and legally.

About the Author

Joan L Green grew up in Santa Monica, California. After leaving California, she traveled extensively and also lived in Connecticut, Texas, and Florida. She now lives in Las Vegas, Nevada. She studied journalism in college, and she used to write feature stories for the local newspaper in Florida. Her passion is investigating corporate fraud, and she used her journalistic skills in writing this book. She is now working on a second book on corporate corruption. In 1997, she appeared on national television on Rivera Live. At that time, Geraldo Rivera was on vacation, and John Gibson interviewed her. She also appeared on AM Live in Philadelphia. She loves to hear firsthand personal experiences from people who have dealt with corporate fraud and corruption. If you have any experiences to tell, go to her website, www.JoanLGreen.com, and share your story. It might be the next one to be investigated and used in her next book.